THE WORSHIPING LIFE

THE WORSHIPING LIFE
Meditations on the Order of Worship

Lisa Nichols Hickman

WESTMINSTER
JOHN KNOX PRESS
LOUISVILLE · KENTUCKY

Book design by Sharon Adams
Cover design by Pam Poll Graphic Design
Cover art: Bob Commander / Images.com

First edition
Published by Westminster John Knox Press
Louisville, Kentucky

This book is printed on acid-free paper that meets the American National Standards Institute Z39.48 standard. ∞

PRINTED IN THE UNITED STATES OF AMERICA

05 06 07 08 09 10 11 12 13 14—10 9 8 7 6 5 4 3 2 1

Library of Congress Cataloging-in-Publication Data

Hickman, Lisa Nichols.
    The worshiping life / by Lisa Nichols Hickman—1st ed.
        p. cm.
    Includes bibliographical references.
    ISBN 0-664-22759-7 (alk. paper)
    1. Public worship—Presbyterian Church (U.S.A.)—Meditations. 2. Presbyterian Church (U.S.A.)—Liturgy—Meditations. I. Title.

BX8969.5.H53 2005
264'.051—dc22   2004050889

To my grandparents,
Bob and Agnes Nichols

Contents

Acknowledgments

I am grateful first and foremost to the pastors who have shaped my worshiping life, beginning with my dad, Lee Nichols, and continuing through a long line of fine preachers, pastors and administrators. I am thankful to Gray Norsworthy, Tom Kort, Alice Johnston, David Prince, Lou Kilgore, Clarence Ammons, Jean Seitz, Joy Kulvicki, David A. Davis, Lauren McFeaters, Mark Orten, Joyce Mackichan Walker, Fred Wood, Valerie Moore and Betty May Seel, for the ways they brought worship to life both in the sanctuary and in their own worshiping lives. A special thank you to Carol Freebairn and Lois Eggers for their support of two of these congregations through their love and their administrative duties.

The life of worship happens within a body of believers. I am grateful to the congregations of Highland Presbyterian Church in Baton Rouge, Louisiana; Woodlawn Presbyterian Church in St. Louis, Missouri; Sardis Presbyterian Church in Charlotte, North Carolina; First Presbyterian Church of Ewing, New Jersey; Nassau Presbyterian Church in Princeton, New Jersey; and Immanuel Presbyterian Church in Tucson, Arizona.

Thank you to my parents—Lynn and Steve Dull, Warren and Cinda Hickman, Lee and Deb Nichols—for your love and support. Thank you to my siblings—Rob and Mette Nichols, Brenda Hickman, Gary and Maureen Swanson—for their encouragement and good humor.

The writing of this book would not have been possible without the support of the Lilly Endowment, who provided a grant through its Valparaiso Project on the Education and Formation of the People in

Faith. I am particularly thankful to Dorothy Bass, Don Richter and Susan Briehl for their encouragement of this project.

As part of this grant, several small groups from Tucson congregations gathered to discuss their own lives of worship. I am appreciative for small groups from Immanuel Presbyterian Church, the Presbyterian Ministry at the University of Arizona, Valley Presbyterian Church and Mosaic Methodist Church. Those who participated did so with a vulnerability and honesty that brought life to this project. Thank you.

This book was born in the desert, which looked a little prickly upon first arrival. While water rarely poured out from the sky, friendships nourished the dry ground and helped this book to grow. Thank you to Katherine Rodenkirch, Sue Arnpriester, Mary Fernandez, Lisa Goeller, Angela Bordonaro, Katie Holton and Courtney Dodge. Thank you to Jen Roberts for her keen eye and theological insight in serving as in-town editor. A special thank you to Teresa Blythe for her wisdom and expertise. Also thanks to Fran, Cicely and Mari, who provided not just hours of babysitting, but lots of love for our daughter. Other friends who provided encouragement from the very beginning I am deeply indebted to: Cathy Clasen, Chrissie Knight, Elizabeth Clark Thasiah, Robin Keegan, Deborah Barkley, Jamie Consuegra, Mary Rodgers, Abby Heinrich Sydnor and Jon Paul Sydnor.

A special thank you to the Tucson-Pima County Public Library, the San Francisco Theological Seminary and its library staff, Eden Theological Seminary and its library staff, and Princeton Theological Seminary and its library staff.

Thank you to David Dobson, Tom Long, and Daniel Braden for their faithfulness in editing and support.

Finally, to my husband, Jason, thank you for introducing me to the life of worship as lived out through poetry and prayer. To Leah, and our daughter on her way, I give thanks to God for a life with you that is continually "shocking and amazing" as we discover new things together.

Prelude

The Lord said:
Because these people draw near me
with their mouths and honor me with their lips,
while their hearts are far from me,
and their worship of me is a human commandment
learned by rote;
so I will again do amazing things with this people,
shocking and amazing.
—Isaiah 29:13–14b

Gathering

Gathering

Still the god remains an ever-growing
wholeness we have irritably burst.
We are sharp, for we insist on knowing,
But he exists serenely and dispersed.
    —*Rainer Maria Rilke,*[1] *from "Still the God Remains"*

*O*ne of the greatest gatherings in the New Testament is described in the feeding of the five thousand. Certainly there was a large crowd gathered, over five thousand. But even more than the gathered crowd, the gathering of the leftover crumbs gives testament to the miraculous. The disciples were growing irritable that day. Long on the road, wearied from the crowds, ready for a good night's rest, hungry, they encouraged Christ to send the crowd gathered to the surrounding villages to find provisions. Christ would not be swayed by sensibility. "You give them something to eat," he calmly replied. With irritability, about to burst, the disciples cried, "But . . . we have just five loaves and two fish!" We know the end of the story.

Some people try to take the miracle out of the story. Maybe they only started with five loaves and two fish, and in the sharing those gathered felt moved to open up their picnic baskets and share as well. Perhaps the Gospel writer got caught up in the miracle himself. Maybe he exaggerated a little, some commentators suggest. Personally, I don't know why we have a problem believing this miracle story. If we claim Christ as Lord and Savior, acknowledging his teaching and healing ministry, then we better be ready to embrace all of his miracles as well. I know five thousand were fed that day by five loaves and two fish. In my years in the ministry, I've seen such miracles of provision and multiplication take place.

The detail in the story that leaves me scratching my head comes at the very end. The disciples are irritable, understandably. Feet dusty and blistered, they are tired and ready for rest. On top of the physical strain is this whirlwind spiritual journey. They've been caught in Christ's net and haven't had time to stop and think about all the wonder that had transpired. In the midst of the demands of discipleship, when did they have time to stop and reflect? Pray? Worship?

Knowing a deeper need than their physical need, Christ ignores their pleas for rest and gives them one last task before a break. Those who had gathered had eaten their fill. After the feast, not one single bread crumb was left for the birds, because the disciples were asked by Christ to gather them up by hand. As Luke 9:17 confirms, "What was left was gathered up, twelve baskets of broken pieces." The Gospels of Matthew and Mark agree in this important detail.

Anyone who has gathered crumbs knows that it is backbreaking work. Bent over, legs aching, minds dizzy, crumb by crumb filling a basket would take an hour of work. Why gather the crumbs? Certainly those birds at home on the Sea of Galilee would have loved a late night snack. Certainly the next hungry crowd wouldn't be fed by leftovers; they too deserved the abundance of the miracle. Maybe Christ was concerned with order, but wasn't he the guy who healed on the Sabbath and spit into the mud? These crumbs and their gathering is an important detail in this miracle story.

Maybe Christ knew that gathering crumbs is an act of worship. Perhaps he understood that in the repetitive motions of bending, grasping, lifting, a prayerful frame of mind emerges even amid the weariness and irritability. Here in the midst of one of the greatest gatherings depicted in the biblical witness, Christ shows us a new way of understanding our call as disciples to pick up the crumbs.

My days are filled with crumbs. As a mother of an eighteen-month-old, life is all about graham cracker crumbs, peanut butter and jelly crumbs, Goldfish crumbs. It's easy to get irritable day in and day out as I pick up the crumbs over and over again. Mind numb as I bend, grasp, lift over and over again, it's easy to forget a miracle has taken place. Some people look at the crumbs and simply see a mess. What do these have to do with God, faith or worship, they ask. Others look at those fragmented pieces and know that somehow they say something about God. Practicing worship by picking up crumbs is about having the eyes to see, if not the miracle, at least the Maker in the hand of our day-to-day lives. When we see that hand, we are called to worship.

Christ's call to gather the crumbs was a call to worship. It was a call to remember what had taken place that day—the gathering of thousands, the proclaiming that all will be fed, the responding of one willing to share five loaves and two fish, the sealing by the Holy Spirit in the blessing and breaking and giving it out aplenty to those gathered, the bearing out into the world of five thousand fed and filled people. Bend, grasp, lift, place in the basket. A miracle took place this evening. Bend, grasp, lift, place in the basket. Five thousand were nourished by five loaves and two fish. In this repetitive act, worship happened as the disciples gathered around the Word and gathered up his crumbs.

We might feel as if we need to walk into worship free of crumbs—cleaned up, pressed and dressed—ready for the service of God. But God asks us to gather up the crumbs and carry them in with us. Don't brush them off or leave them behind. Gather up the crumbs of your life; stuff them into your pockets if you don't have a basket nearby. Haul them in with a wagon; just don't leave them behind. Pastor Fred Wood invites, "The reason we have thick legs on our Communion table is so that it can handle the weight of all the stuff we carry in. What a shame it would be if we carried the weight of it all the way to church and then carried the weight of it all home with us again. We've got to leave it here at the table."

In worship we gather up the crumbs, and in our gathering we are reminded that a miracle has taken place. We pick up the day-to-dayness of our lives and give it to God as an offering. "Tranform this, bless this, use this," we plead. We haul in our calendars, report cards, financial statements, grocery lists and to-do lists. We carry our palm pilots, daytimers, calendars and appointment books. We bring in the stuff we have done and the stuff we have left undone. Whether we know it or not, we carry in our family stories and histories and secrets and sadness. We bring in our preoccupations and our occupations, our hopes and our failures. Life can feel pretty crummy sometimes, and yet we are still called to worship. We are called to this gathering that somehow helps put the pieces back together. If God exists, as Rilke writes, somewhat serenely and dispersed, then isn't part of our task as believers gathering it all up so that somehow in the midst of the pieces coming together God might be revealed?

In the movie *One True Thing*, Meryl Streep plays Katherine, a mother battling cancer. Early in the movie she is excited for a fall family gathering. Golden leaves blanket the sidewalks that welcome home her daughter, Ellen, who is coming home for her father's birthday. The invitation is to come dressed in costume. Ellen, however, comes dressed in black, clearly having given no thought to a costume. Not even the red shoes of the mother's Dorothy costume from *The Wizard of Oz* can click away the disappointment she feels. From the beginning, this gathering isn't going as planned. As Katherine sets aside her disappointment and continues the party preparations, it is clear there is tension between mother and daughter. In Ellen's half-hearted attempt to help her mother, a plate goes flying off the counter and breaks into many pieces. Its shattering is a reminder that the gathering isn't going well.

This could be the picture of almost any family or church supper scene. Expectations abound. Hopes are high. There is an eagerness to gather and connect. Yet we live with those shattering reminders that all is not perfect. We are human. We let other people down. We fail to live up to the invitation and the expectation. Things shatter. And yet we worship.

In the movie, Katherine doesn't just sweep the broken pieces of the plate into the trash. She asks her daughter to pick them up and save them. For Katherine there is something important about these pieces. Later in the film we see that Katherine has a vision for these broken pieces. Weak from radiation treatment, she picks up the pieces and arranges them into a mosaic. This is clearly a prayerful time.

Our worship is about picking up the pieces, whether the pieces are soft and crumbly or jagged and sharp. These are the broken pieces of the body of Christ, and they need rearranging. We build these pieces into one and offer them up to the one and only true thing. In picking up the pieces, we know unfailingly that a miracle has taken place. We worship because we know life can feel crummy. We worship because we live amid crumbs. We worship because we know in God there is a wholeness greater than the pieces of our lives. We worship because we are sharp and life can be shattered, and yet God's serene nature beckons us in. In our worship we pick up all of this stuff, set it at the table and know that God alone is the one true thing.

The gathering isn't just about us and our crumbs. We gather in community around the Word of God. That Word is Christ himself, the one who became crumbs so we could have a foretaste of God's kingdom. That Word is also the Scripture giving witness to the life of Christ, from the gathering of crumbs in the manna in the wilderness to Paul's proclamation that he feels like a crumb himself; we gather around these words and are filled and fed.

We gather to muster up the courage to confess. We gather to join voices with others when ours are lacking, to sing praise and sing lament. We gather to be strengthened to go out into the world and live a life faithful to the gospel. We gather to be challenged to do justice, love kindness and walk humbly with our God. We gather to be assured that we are forgiven and loved. We gather to bless, confess and address the injustices of our world. We gather because life is hard and we find strength in community and hope in our faith.

Several years ago a young college student died suddenly in a car accident. Her roommate Sarah worshiped in the congregation of a pastor named John. Sarah expressed her grief to her pastor, who wrote her a letter. "Dear Sarah," he began, "I know you must be feeling pretty angry at God. Why did this happen? Why did my best friend have to die? I know you must have a thousand questions and I am sure you have shed even more tears. God did not want your friend to die. God is there crying and asking why with you." He sent the letter and never heard back from Sarah. He wondered if it had made a difference.

A decade later, John died in a car crash. His wife, shattered by the loss of her best friend and crushed by facing the future alone, slowly tried to pick up the pieces. Anne arranged the funeral, took care of the finances and maintained a stoic face through it all. Finally she sat down one day to sort the junk mail, pay the bills and read the growing stack of cards. She was surprised when she opened up one card and a carefully folded letter fell out from its fold. You might say it even looked like a crumb. As she unfolded the letter, Anne gasped when she realized it was John's handwriting.

The card said, "I received this letter from your husband ten years ago when my college roommate died. You can see from its tears and stains I have read this letter many times. I thought this letter should be in your hands now. It gave me hope then, I hope it gives you comfort now." And then Anne read again, "Why did my best friend have to die?"

There are times in our lives when all we can see are the broken pieces, and yet the miracle is there. Worship calls us to gather the crumbs prayerfully, attend to Christ's presence in the gathering, offer them to God and see what is proclaimed from there.

The disciples were irritable about having to gather up the crumbs. They were exhausted and ready to rest their weary feet. Twelve baskets later, the land once filled with bread crumbs was clear again. As the disciples gathered those crumbs, they had no idea of the crumbs they would be called to pick up just a few years down the line. They too would lose their best friend. Hopes of a kingdom would be shattered. Their visions of peace would be in pieces. The crumbs they had to pick up after the death of Jesus were much more than a clearing littered with bread crumbs. They had to pick up the crumbs of shattered hopes and a misunderstood Messiah. They had lost not only their friend, but more importantly, their teacher, master, savior, and Lord. Yet they were called to worship, to build the church piece by piece from this point on. Their gathering paved the way for our worship. Are we ready to gather the crumbs and begin the worshiping life?

Call to Worship

You do not have to be good.
You do not have to walk on your knees
for a hundred miles through the desert, repenting.
You only have to let the soft animal of your body love what
*   it loves.*
Tell me about despair, yours, and I will tell you mine.
Meanwhile the world goes on.
Meanwhile the sun and the clear pebbles of the rain
are moving across the landscapes,
over the prairies and the deep trees,
the mountains and the rivers.
Meanwhile the wild geese, high in the clean blue air,
are heading home again.
Whoever you are, no matter how lonely,
the world offers itself to your imagination,
calls to you like the wild geese, harsh and exciting—
over and over announcing your place
in the family of things.
                                    —Mary Oliver, "Wild Geese"[1]

*L*ast fall, in the midst of the peak season, I invited a friend for a walk to soak in the last of the fall leaves. She in turn invited a friend, an artist and gallery owner. We set out on a street, busier than we normally liked to walk on, but this particular street was canopied in light-soaked leaves of yellow, red and orange. We walked with our heads up, trying to carry on a conversation, but lost in the beauty of the late afternoon. It was the time of day in October when the sun shines down at just the right angle and everything glows in protracted light. We watched birds fly in drunken mobs, as if they imbibed too much light and color in the trees that they flocked to over and over again. Then, above the spinning of the wheels around us, we heard the cries of the wild geese. Flying in V formation, focused in direction, familiar with the routines of the season, their cries made us stop in our tracks.

I was overwhelmed by the perfection of the late afternoon. All creation was joining together in praise and in glory. But I stood there like a stolid Presbyterian. No leaping or dancing, just an earthbound pedestrian. It was the artist, the gallery owner, who responded to the call. She raised her arms, cupped her hands, tilted her head back and drank it all in. She couldn't get enough, nor could she offer up enough thanksgiving for that moment. Her uninhibited praise, the beauty of the day and the cry of the wild geese called me to worship. In that moment I knew my place in this family of things—it was to glorify God and enjoy God forever.

The first time the world offered itself so much to my imagination that it sparked a call to worship was in high school. It was a school trip with the drama class to the local theater company, a much-needed break from the roar of the routine at the high school. The play was called "The Diviners." As the curtains opened, a teenaged boy stumbled across the stage with a divining stick searching for water. I couldn't tell you the whole story today. I can only remember the boy with the stick searching for water and my response. As the curtain closed and the audience clapped, tears flowed down my face. Embarrassed by the outpouring of emotion splashed across my face, I grew nervous as the houselights flickered on. Yet that moment was a moment where I was called to worship. I understood the boy's search for that life-giving water. And I recognized the tremble in his stick. I was called to worship because I knew his thirst.

Most days the call to worship isn't quite so clear and I'm not quite so open. Days become routine and habits engrained. My daytimer doesn't leave much space to be called out of what needs to be done. Does the routine create space for God to break in, or does the routine attempt to block God out? My need for control and my own self-centeredness aren't really conducive to being called away from them to another form of worship. Are the interruptions to our schedules God's call, or do we merely see them as inconvenience?

Recently I set out on a hike hoping to reach the top of the mountain and to have reflection away from the routine, but that moment of peace lasted only as long as the bugs stayed away. A few bites and I was back down the mountain. I can't remember the last time I was so called to worship that I was able to forget the distractions and focus solely on God. I need a call so loud that it drowns out the murmurs of what needs to be done that constantly echo in my head. I need a call that isn't just printed words or routine litanies, but an embodied expression of expectation that God might move and we will tremble in the presence of that movement.

Instead of allowing ourselves the opportunity to be called to worship in any time and place, we call upon God to meet us on our time lines. We want God to move within our guidelines. In his book *Bobos in Paradise*, David Brooks comments firsthand on the predicament of the twenty-first-century seeker:

> I'm sitting on a rock in the Big Blackfoot River in western Montana. The sun is glistening off the water, and the grasses on the banks are ablaze in their fall glory. The air is crisp and silent and I am utterly alone. . . . This is the spot where Norman Maclean set and Robert Redford filmed "A River Runs Through It," and I'm sitting here waiting for one of those perfect moments when time stops and I feel myself achieving a mystical communion with nature. But nothing's happening. I've been hanging around this magnificent setting for 30 minutes and I haven't had one moment of elevated consciousness. The ageless rhythms of creation are happening all around me. The crisp air whispers. The branches sway. The ducks wing by silently . . . I look at my watch and realize I had better start feeling serene oneness with God's creation pretty soon. I've got dinner reservations back in Missoula at six.[2]

Our reservations limit much more than the possibility of encountering God—they prevent us from being called to a new and exciting place, a new way of worship where both in and out of the sanctuary we sense the movement of God.

We gather for worship because each of us hopes to be called out of our stuck places and into a new way of living. We want to worship without reservations. We come seeking a sip of that life-giving water. We come with divining sticks in hand hoping they will tremble and tell us where to dig deep. We come, some of us, with arms raised ready to receive what is offered, while others come clenched but hopeful. We come hoping our imaginations will be sparked. We come in our loneliness. We come with our despair, some ready to tell and others ready to listen. We come repenting. We come wanting to know how we fit into this family of things.

The call to worship, offered in the service of worship, gathers all of these disparate elements together and sets us all before God. The call to worship has the difficult task of gathering us all together from our individual preoccupations and calling to mind that we are here for God, not for ourselves. The call to worship must excite and enlarge, invoke and impress. Its task is paradoxical. It anchors and propels. It must acknowledge where we are at, and at the same time refuse our remaining in that place. It is simultaneously an invitation and a rejection. The call to worship must break both the silence of our aloneness and the giddy chatter of our eagerness to connect. And it must acknowledge loudly and clearly that many things call to us for our worship, but it is God alone to whom we ultimately bow.

More days than not, I feel like the birds that fly chaotically through the sky—this way and that—rather than purposefully like the geese. Ordered and directed, the goal of the geese is clear and their movements succinct. They are headed home. I flit around from this to that because so many things call out for my worship. I need a call that is decisive and loud. It might even need to sound harsh in challenging the status quo of the day. I need it to order my life with the structure of liturgy and direct my thoughts to the only one worthy of my worship. Gather us in perfect V formation, God, and lead us home to you.

Luke, Hannah and Chris, three middle-schoolers, offered one of the most undeniable calls to worship I have ever heard. It was "spontaneous" worship night—a favorite activity in middle-school fellowship. It was a favorite for me as well because it required only the imagination of the group gathered. We would divide into varying groups to prepare the call to worship, prayers of confession, sermon, prayers of the people and the offering. Each group was given a Scripture verse, the theme for the evening and a creative prop that might be used.

One night during Epiphany, using the call of Isaiah, "Arise, shine, for your light has come!" and using glow-in-the-dark stars, balloons, neon glow sticks and crepe streamers, we broke up into groups to put together the worship service. Twenty minutes later, we gathered in the sanctuary not knowing exactly what would take place. Luke stood in the pulpit. "Arise, shine, your light has come!" he proclaimed with all of his might. We all smiled at his earnestness and energy. Then, out from under the pulpit, surprising us all, jumped Chris. "Go God!" he exclaimed while throwing and unrolling crepe streamers.

Luke went on with the call to worship: "See darkness covers the earth and thick darkness the people." Then came another surprise from behind the pulpit, but this time it was a whisper. Hannah, with black crepe streamers, rose up and whispered, "We know the darkness." With such words of truth uttered by young tongues, we couldn't help but be drawn to worship. After a moment of strange silence, we looked up, and there in the balcony was the rest of their group rising up from their hiding places and lifting their arms up over their heads. Streamers in hand, they shook them with all their might and yelled in unison, "God, we're here to worship. Now show us the way."

If all calls to worship both in worship and in our lives had such an urgency to them, there would be no way we could remain stolid, stiff and separated. In no way would we remain pedestrian or reserved; we would be provoked to praise. We know the darkness, but we're here. We carry despair, mine and yours, but we've come to worship. We know we are part of a bigger family of things, though we don't know how to embrace it; but we gather together and try. Show us the way, Lord, whether it's by unrolling streamers, exciting our imaginations, screaming into our ears or whispering gently. Yank our hands, Lord, and drag us past our reservations toward a revelation of the way you call us to worship this very day.

Prayer of Invocation

Upon adventure promised seas
Sailed unfurled the mariners' pride
Trojan ship of surpassing speed
As siren before a salt shroud bride

Resplendent were her prow and masts
Adorned by captive hearts of men
Honored she, Poseidon's Queen
So fair the minstrel musings rang

Yet in the swell one star lit eve
As waters danced celestial gold
The seamen's eyes wandered deep
And foundered upon light untold

Out of legion's yawning night
Drew sight, ere else grew dim
And voice of gentle, primordial speak
Filled the mind and heart within

"Come My own, forsake the lee
And brave the leviathan quest.
Dive! Into My quenching fathomless sea
Which is my pierc'ed breast."

—*Elizabeth Clark Thasiah,*
"Upon Adventure"[1]

*T*he primordial is at the very depths of the worshiping life. A voice gentle and primal calls us to something beyond ourselves, invoking worship and prompting praise. We listen, sometimes knowingly and sometimes not, for that whisper which calls us to jump into the deep. "Dive!" it says, and we can either hold our breath and plunge into the depths or stay in the boat. We whisper back to that gentle voice, praying for courage and direction. When we sense its absence, we pray to invoke the very presence of God. When we sense its presence, we pray for courage to face the challenge that the voice of God invokes within us. Our prayers of invocation are prayers that stir up the primordial deep, asking the voice of God to speak and to fill our minds and hearts within.

Often we Christians do not take prayers of invocation seriously. We say it's because we as humans do not have the power to do any work that might bring grace, but I think that's an excuse. Invoking the presence of God means inviting God's Spirit to be turned loose upon us. God on the loose might demand us to change, challenge us to reprioritize, call us to true repentance. Do we really want to leave worship different than we came in? We are much more comfortable with adoration rather than invocation. Ascribing lofty words of adoration and exaltation acknowledges, yes, that we are creatures. But it affirms even more so that we are cowards. Give Christianity a real try? Are we ready for that? God on the loose, God's presence truly invoked, might mean we dive into the depths of our days a little differently.

A prayer of invocation is offered to summon the presence of God in the worship service. This is tricky territory because it isn't a wave of a magic wand, a hocus-pocus abracadabra: POW! God is magically present. God isn't a vision we can conjure up with mirrors and smoke and sleight of hand. Nor does God depend on us to be invited to the party. God is the guest of honor whether invited or not. Some might even deem the prayer of invocation unnecessary because "wherever two or three are gathered in my name, I am there among them" (Matt. 18:20). Yet out of honor for God and humility as creatures, we pray for invocation. We pray for invocation because we are all too capable of re-voking God's presence—we retract from worship, rescind our invitations for God's presence in our lives and repel any notion that we depend on God. It is because of this tendency to revoke that we invoke: God, speak from the depths and draw us out of ourselves.

Most might not even recognize the difference between a prayer of adoration and a prayer of invocation. They are both about God—isn't that enough? But in my day-to-day life, there is a big difference. Each day when I am faced with the challenge of the day—with the depths that call out for me to dive into, the ledge that awaits my leap, the setting forth in faith to serve as I might—each time I am faced with those areas of darkness I want to avoid, I am much more apt to ask for God's Spirit to be set loose rather than going on about how great God is.

As a pastor, the times I most often find myself saying a prayer of invocation are when I knock on a hospital door. This past spring, a rattlesnake in the canyon near our home bit a young girl of four, who was out for a special day with her mom. The day drew grim in the fearful moments of finding a phone in the wilderness, awaiting the ambulance and praying the antivenin would be at the hospital. Antivenin is a precious thing and at times difficult to find. Not all hospitals are able to stock it. After arriving at the hospital, the girl was given the antivenin and then given it again and again. A normal dose of antivenin for an adult bitten by a snake is eight to ten vials. The severity of this snakebite was so great it required forty-eight vials. Needless to say, young Emma's life was at stake as they waited to see if the serum would work.

I had seen the story unfold on the midday news, but I was surprised when the phone rang and I found out that Emma was the granddaughter of members of my former church across the country in New Jersey. "Would you go and visit the family in the hospital? She is in critical condition."

Now, my husband, also a pastor, is at his best in these kinds of situations. But for me, responding to a crisis like this is like jumping into the deep. I have to muster up all the courage I can and call upon the resources of past dives. It is in that moment of absolute fear of the unknown where I whisper those words of invocation, "Turn yourself loose here, Lord. I cannot do it alone. I cannot do it at all, not without you by my side." It's not a grand prayer, but it's an honest invoking.

As we cry out in worship in need of God's invocation, we open ourselves to the evocation and provocation that can arise only from God: to be inspired, reawakened, called out from our preoccupation with ourselves. In that evocation, we are reminded of our earliest memories of God's love and trust. At the same time we ask to be provoked so that something within us might be stirred to action, perhaps even angered by the state of the world, and from there we might be called forth to a new way of living. The prayers of invocation are prayers for God's presence right here and now in this time and place in this moment of eternal now. Buttressing that prayer are the past and the future—an evocation of our past knowledge and a provocation that our future world might be different due to a change in our actions. These waves of time lap at our toes—past knowledge, present need, future change—and invite us in.

A prayer of invocation is a jump into those waves. It is not a passive, distant pastime, but a willingness to jump into the current of God's activity in the world. It is this prayer of invocation, uttered from the very beginning of our worship, that asks that God be unleashed not just in our worship, but in our very life of prayer itself. Here we are warming up, mustering up the courage to dive in. The most important question that buoys the invocation is whether we are ready for the consequences. If we dare invoke the presence of God, we need to be ready and willing to honor God's arrival. If we are not ready to be swept into the waves, then why pray for invocation? If the sanctuary were a log ride at an amusement park, the majority of the congregation would not get splashed in the front seats of the ride. If we are more comfortable in the back seats where we barely get a dribble of that refreshing water, are we really ready to invoke the presence of God? Annie Dillard is often quoted:

> Does anyone have the foggiest idea what sort of power we blithely invoke? Or, as I suspect, does no one believe a word of it? The churches are children playing on the floor with their chemistry sets, mixing up a batch of TNT to kill a Sunday morning. It is madness to wear ladies' straw hats and velvet hats to church; we should all be wearing crash helmets. Ushers should issue life preservers and signal flares; they should lash us to our pews. For the sleeping god

may wake someday and take offense, or the waking god may draw us out to where we can never return.[2]

When I pray for invocation, I pray that the waking God might draw me out so that I wouldn't be lashed to the pew or those places of fear in my life, but that I might be called to a new way of living out the gospel. At its root, "invocation" comes from *vocare,* meaning "to call." In the prayer of invocation, we call God into our game of life. We are saying we don't want a passive God on the sidelines, but a God who plays offense and defense on our team.

It was in the calling into being of the generations, beginning with Adam and Eve, that the name of God was first invoked. In the birth of generations, "people began to invoke the name of the Lord" (Gen. 4:26). There was the darkness of death in those days as well, Abel at the hand of Cain, and yet people began to summon the name of the Lord. We call upon the name of God because God is the one who "invokes" us—God is the one who calls us into being. As the waves of the generations ebb and flow, as the tides of tender love and awful bloodshed crash together, people continue to invoke the name of the Lord.

Last summer my husband and I were enjoying a quintessential summer day—a day at the Jersey shore. There at Spring Lake, in between rocky jetties, is the perfect place to ride the waves. After a day enjoying coasting in on the current, we were waterlogged and exhausted. Taking one last ride on a wave, we collapsed on the beach. If we had not rested then we would have missed what happened next. A man of about ninety, suited up in bright yellow swim trunks, eagerly approached the water accompanied by what appeared to be his two sons helping him balance on either side. He did not look strong, and it was clear from the gasps on the beach that many were concerned as he walked out into the strong waves. He and his sons waded into the water, all the time looking ahead at the waves crashing in front of them. All of a sudden, as a wave came crashing at their chests, the man dove headfirst into it. Those watching as he disappeared anxiously awaited his reappearance. We wondered how his sons could let him go under. After those lengthy seconds of concern, his head popped out of the water and he turned around to face his sons. There on his face was the largest smile I have ever seen on a person of any age.

Because we must find our way through the darkness, because every decision is a ledge and our beings are always on the precipice of death, we have no other whisper within us that is capable of salvation but that whispered prayer of invocation. Once we have let it escape from our lips, then we sit and wait for the signs. We sit and wait for our emergence from the waves and the emergent smile in discovering their joy. Life can be cold and black and tumultuous, yet there is always the God who draws us up from the deep. Our toes touch that cold, black wave and often we retreat. Yet God calls us, invokes us, to dive in and emerge smiling.

Once he emerged, it was clear that if the man's sons had denied his desire to dive in, they would have revoked his invocation. His jumping in, diving in headfirst, was a sign of trust. But it was his emergence from the deep with such joy that I will always remember. He invoked for me the presence of God through his joy and his trust. What a starting place for prayer. What a diving into worship. We may not have yellow swim trunks, but we do have the deep waves surrounding us. Do we dare dive into the primordial deep?

Opening Hymn

"The song that I came to sing remains unsung to this day. I have spent my days in stringing and unstringing my instrument."
—*Rabindranath Tagore,*
"The song that I came to sing"[1]

What if Mary had waited until she found perfect pitch to sing the Magnificat? What if David had been so busy stringing and unstringing his lyre that there were no such thing as the book of Psalms? What if Zechariah, Elizabeth's husband, had been unable to sing? Mute at the sound of the angel's prophecy, a song certainly wouldn't come easily. But what if when his tongue was loosed, he had been so self-consumed he had forgotten to pause and offer a song of thanksgiving? Certainly the biblical page would become more linear and less lyrical, but even more so the biblical story would lose some of its panache and transcendence. These songs are verses that magnify God's glory because there is truth in Augustine's words, "Whoever sings, prays twice." The amplification comes from the embodiment of the prayer, and we know without a doubt that the God who comes in the form of Jesus Christ likes stuff made in the flesh. A verse reverberates in the nerve endings that otherwise are untapped. A note knows a different part of us than a simple word does.

No one knows this better than the writer of Luke's Gospel. Who needs Broadway or community theater when we have this in our hands? Strike up the band; here come Mary and Zechariah, the angel chorus and Simeon too. These folks aren't sitting around stringing their instruments; they are ready when the Spirit moves to belt their hearts out. "Start spreading the news," they practically sing out; take note that something new is happening here. The writer of the Gospel of Mark started a new genre—the Gospel. What kind of genre is the book of Luke? It's a story told in song.

So if the story strikes up a tune, why am I so hesitant to sing it out sometimes? Certainly I don't have the best voice. The folks who suffered the most at the sound of my voice were in the wedding party at which I officiated when the organist started the chords for the first hymn to sing, and no one picked up their hymnals. There in the front of the sanctuary, miked so all could hear, I had my first karaoke experience, my first live, on-stage solo act. Nothing unsung here; they heard every off-key note. The reason I hesitate to sing is really because I hesitate to be transformed. Singing transforms word into wonder, and there are days when I would much rather sit around stringing and unstringing my instrument than face transformation.

Sundays after church, even after worship had ended, my mom would keep singing. Fixing lunch in the kitchen, running errands that afternoon, working out in the yard, the hymns continued. "Surely it is God who saves me," she would sing as she diced onions and peppers for jambalaya. "And he will raise me up on eagle's wings," she would hum as she pruned the bushes in our backyard. On those Sundays growing up, I was more caught up in adolescent anxieties than a new tune. I fretted about guys; I was consumed by my appearance. I'd rather be out at the mall with my allowance looking for the next best thing to buy. In other words, there was a lot about me that was unsung. The counterpoint to my song was my mom's voice, which brought joy and prayer to our home. Mary may have sung the Magnificat, but my mom's song seemed to proclaim, "I like my life a lot." I learned from her tune.

The writer of Luke holds the microphone up to folks like my mom who sing out in their lives. The first solo is Mary's song: "My soul magnifies the Lord, and my spirit rejoices in God my savior, for he has looked with favor on the lowliness of his servant. Surely from now on all generations will call me blessed." The listener knows that this last verse is the most unbelievable of all. For her to believe that other generations might remember this pregnant teen is inconceivable.

Countless musicians over the centuries have tried to put a tune to Mary's song. All of the greatest composers like Bach, Vivaldi, Schubert, Mozart, Tallis and Pachelbel tried. Discovering an ancient text with the chords actually recorded would be an unbelievable find. Until then, musicians are left to exegete the meaning of the text through chord and instrument. Their challenge is greater than that of the theologians who try to exegete the text as well. It is hard to even imagine what the true tune would add to this text because even in just the words themselves Mary expresses an inner harmony over and against the outer discord of her situation and her world. No stringing and unstringing for Mary; she didn't have the luxury of time or the relaxation of a settled place to do so. No time for adolescent anxiety. Mary belted out the Magnificat, in full voice, because whether or not she was ready, an even greater song was about to be born.

What the Gospel of Luke says is to listen to voices like these, the marginalized and forgotten, and to listen deeply to their voices. In the novel *Bell Canto*, Roxanne Coss is an opera singer of exquisite pitch and inconceivable range. A birthday party is thrown for a powerful Japanese businessman, and dignitaries around the world have gathered to witness his gift, an aria sung by Roxanne herself. In the course of the party, the unthinkable happens when revolutionaries seize hold of the home and hold the guests hostage. The story unfolds to examine how this beautiful song finds text and tune in the community formed by dignitaries and radical revolutionaries.

While it would be easy to assume that it is her beautiful voice that gives the book its title, there is one voice, marginalized and forgotten, that sings out midway through the book. Having listened to and observed Roxanne for months, one young terrorist enters the gathering and starts to sing. Suddenly it's unclear whose voice gives the title its name. What is poignant about the book and his beautiful voice is that we know that once the hostages are released this voice could easily be lost due to circumstance and lack of privilege. It is unfathomable that this song could go unsung, not because of his preoccupation with stringing and unstringing his instrument, but because of the unfair ways the world has been strung together.

Then Luke tells us, singing at times, that the world is going to be restrung. "Start spreading the news"—someone is coming who will hold a microphone up to all those voices that have gone unheard. It is these voices that will be the instruments God will use in the ongoing chorus of redemption. When we hear that chord of God's grace, the discord of God's world becomes more resonant, but at the same time we are challenged to bring the world into accord with God's vision of a new kingdom.

The band U2 is one of the best bands of our time. Born out of broken Northern Ireland, their music longs for reconciliation and peace. Bono, the lead singer, has the wonderful life of success and the luxury of fortune. He has the time and the resources to spend as much time stringing and unstringing his guitar as he could ever want. But instead of sitting stagnant, Bono has taken up the task of working to do a little repairing of our world. Raising awareness for AIDS in Africa he has met with people of power and fortune to draw their attention to the growing crisis. I wonder if, working diligently, he has gained strength and courage from Psalm 40. He and his band do a version of this song as a closing benediction at their concerts. It has become a prayer and anthem for many: "I waited patiently for the Lord; he inclined to me and heard my cry. He drew me up from the desolate pit, and out of the miry bog, and set my feet upon a rock, making my steps secure. He put a new song in my mouth, a song of praise to our God. Many will see and fear, and put their trust in the Lord."

In a recent cover article in *Time*, Bono said, "When you sing, you make people vulnerable to change in their lives. You make yourself vulnerable to change in your life. But in the end, you've got to become the change you want to see in the world."[2] In other words, stop stringing yourself and the world along and start singing a new song as you lead a changed life.

Mary sings in the Magnificat a new song, to a child yet unseen, yet to be born, yet to change the world. In the meantime, she sings on. Friends of ours were expecting their first child to be born around Christmas. Shortly after conception, in those warm early summer days of June, the father began singing a Christmas carol to his child each night. "Silent night, holy night, all is calm, all is bright, round yon virgin, mother and child, holy infant so tender and mild, sleep in heavenly peace, sleep in heavenly peace," he would sing each evening as he rested his cheek on the growing tummy of his wife. As she would turn in early, exhausted from the physical labor of growing a child and preparing to give birth, the father would pick up his guitar and play. He played through the summer, through the fall and into the Advent season. When contractions began, he had the presence of mind to put his guitar in the car with them.

After delivery, their child cried immediately, as would be expected. They were a little distraught when he continued to cry. The noise of the delivery room, the roar of the doctors and nurses weighing him, were not the music he wanted to hear. His mom tried to comfort him with the lull of her voice, but the crying continued. So his dad pulled out the guitar and began quietly to sing, "Silent night, holy night, all is calm, all is bright, . . ." and the newborn settled into life in this world.

Whether we sing at Advent or in ordinary time, whether we sing in tune or out of tune, no matter if we sing in worship or at the kitchen sink or along with the radios in our cars, we sing to a child, Jesus Christ, yet to be born again into the world. That child will be born into the noise of this earth that is much more ear shattering than a delivery room. There is the noise of violence in Iraq and Liberia; there is the din of children crying themselves to sleep malnourished at the hand of human ineptitude. Christ will be born into the noise of people who speak constantly instead of putting their words into actions.

It is our task to stop stringing and unstringing our instruments and thereby procrastinating what needs to be done. It is not our instruments that are broken; it is our world that needs fixing. The need is for no song to go unsung and for our voices to join the voices of others in singing this newborn child to still his soul. We are called to sing on and sing on, over and above the noise of this world, a new song to a new child who will ultimately restring the world.

Peter Gomes, chaplain at Harvard University, reminds us, "In [Mary's] call from God and her response to that call, she becomes the mother not only of Jesus but of our vocation, and of our calling as well."[3] Mary sang out. We don't have to be in tune, it might even sound better if we aren't, but we do need to be attuned to the other voices God would have us sing along with. It is the world that is broken, not our instruments; will you procrastinate or will you sing?

Confession

Once upon a time, there was a woman who discovered she had turned into the wrong person.
                    —Anne Tyler, Back When We Were Grownups[1]

*C*acti are a quirky curiosity to me, being new to the desert. From the window of my study I can see the stately saguaro, a tubby barrel cactus and an abundance of prickly pear. For some reason, those cacti call to mind a phrase engrained in childhood. "Give each other warm fuzzies, not cold pricklies." I am not sure if it was taught in Sunday school or used to promote kindheartedness in kindergarten. But I do remember the fuzzy creatures that went with the catchy phrase and the fear of receiving a cold prickly. Those cacti call to mind all those cold pricklies in my life. Though a cactus is anything but cold, its prickly thorns remind me of those moments I have been standoffish, prickly, sinful. The meditation on the cactus thorns is transformed, though, when I pray through those prickly prayers. "Forgive me, God, for the *way* I . . . and *when* I . . . and *how* I. . . . It's funny how the overabundance of "I" begins to look a little prickly.

Cold pricklies may seem inconsequential, but anyone who is familiar with the effect of sin on our lives knows that it is all of the little sins, the countless little lies and the innumerable moments that add up to a whole lot of sin. So comfortable are we with these little imbalances of our lives that we are at a loss when one day they tip over and tumble heavily into our hearts, surprising us when they do begin to prick and poke. I am the wrong person. I don't feel like

27

myself. I am not the person God created me to be. The world might be a better place if I was able to get beyond myself and next to the stranger in my midst. There is something within us that doesn't feel warm, fuzzy, or even cold and prickly—that something feels dead.

Several years ago there was a large and destructive fire at Sabino Canyon, a nature reserve near my home. The fire raged for days, destroying wildlife and plant life alike. Though years later the full damage done is yet to be revealed, the reason so is surprising. The strong saguaro cacti do not die immediately. It takes ten years or more for them to reveal any signs of death. When it does realize its death, as much as a cactus realizes anything, it will slowly begin to shed its skin. Once its skin has been stripped, all that will remain of the cactus are its bare ribs.

Death at times is slow in coming. We wake up one day and realize we are not who we once were. Having experienced three of those moments of recognition in the past few years, I figure I have averaged one death for every ten years of my life. For me those moments come when I am profoundly aware of a place of sin in my life. Sin deadens and kills. It hurts us and those who have to deal with the results of our sin.

Those moments of recognition don't just happen on the individual level; they are corporate as well. The desert landscape is pierced by thorns and so is the landscape of the world. As a church, a nation, a global community, we wake up at times and realize we have died. Corporate dishonesty—a long and slow death. Corruption and abuse in the church—a long and slow death. Communities separated from one another by suburbs stretching out beyond the needs of the inner cities—a long and slow death. Stripped down and ribs beheld bare, our sins are all too apparent, so apparent that we begin to think it is the norm.

There are also the moments when the church wakes up and realizes it doesn't know who it is anymore. This can happen when the church is not able, ready or willing to hear prayers of honest confession. Are we really able to hear and be present to the prayers of confession uttered in absolute honesty? The church is so afraid of hearing and honoring true confession that we limit the ways in which we confess our sin. A call to confession is usually a paragraph-long printed prayer of confession to be read in unison with the corporate body and sixty seconds (the pastor is timing it) of silence to gather your thoughts, name your confessions and be honest about them before God. What if the gathered body had a few *minutes* of silence to sit in honest conversation before God? The prayer of confession intends to pierce the well-protected skin of our sin, to needle us toward honest reflection. But more often than not, this prayer can feel repetitive, rote. It requires an act of the imagination and a deed of courage to take those words and the silence and bring our lives honestly to them. What if the gathered body had a blank section of the bulletin and a pen in hand where the printed prayer had once been? "During this time of confession, write down the places in your life, the actions you have done, the things you have left undone, the people you have harmed. Write these down and then pray over them in a time of silence." In so doing, we might actually internalize our sins, naming them with a sense of ownership for what we have done.

The danger, of course, is that this makes the confession too individual and not a shared corporate prayer. The printed corporate prayers are important because they call to our attention sins we were not even aware we were committing. Recently a local church printed a unison prayer of confession that asked congregants to join together in stating their culpability in these kinds of institutional sins. A woman incensed came up to the pastor after the service: "I didn't come to church to confess those sins—I am not a part of all of that!" But we are. Whether we believe it or not, the institutional sins of racism and economic greed and sexism are all areas we are involved in, and we *do* need to be reminded of that from week to week. That is why we are called to corporate confession so that we name sins beyond our own consuming "I's."

Our prayers of confession need to pierce our hearts and poke our consciences so we can acknowledge the places where we have become the wrong person, and those places where our world has become the wrong world. Big sins and little sins, individual sin and institutional sin—we as human beings are part of it all. We need prayers of confessions that force us to think, that make us honestly evaluate our lives, that call us to confess those sins of commission and the sins of omission. We need prayers of confession with integrity and intentionality because we need something that will call us beyond ourselves. We do not want to admit our own culpability, our own death at times. Annie Dillard tells the story of an Eskimo hunter who went to see the local missionary who had been preaching in his village. "I want to ask you something," the hunter said. "What's that?" responded the missionary. "If I did not know about God and sin," the hunter inquired, "would I go to hell?" "Well no," said the missionary, "not if you did not know!" "Then why," retorted the hunter, "did you tell me?"

We don't want to be told about sin, and we don't want to confess our sins—not in church, not in our daily lives. Yet each Sunday morning at 11:00, like clockwork, we are called to confession for the sin in our lives. Where have you become the wrong person? Where are you dead? What are the small actions you pursue in the day-to-day existence that bring about that cumulative death?

In the movie *Changing Lanes*, two men, played by Ben Affleck and Samuel L. Jackson, have a collision of cars and character that causes a deep need for confession. On one ordinary day, the two are headed separately for appearances before a judge in court. Affleck is to present documents sealing a questionable Wall Street dealing, and Jackson is to argue for custody of his sons. Both are delayed when they crash while changing lanes. Affleck is so hurried that he accidentally drops his important papers, which Jackson finds. The movie unfolds as Affleck seeks to regain the papers. Because Jackson was waylaid by the accident, he was unable to convince the judge of his worthiness to receive partial custody. Angered by the consequences of the crash, Jackson refuses to return the documents. Obstinance turns to revenge, and soon both men are caught up in a cycle of destructive decisions that doesn't take ten years but one terrible day to make them realize they are not who they once were.

In a pivotal scene, Affleck seeks refuge in a church and finds himself in a confessional. Even though the audience sees clearly that he has become the wrong person, he has not owned that for himself. When given an invitation by the priest to confess, he refuses. "No thanks," he says, "I came here for meaning." Yet it is clear to all viewing that Affleck is not going to find any meaning until he opens himself up to the kind of confession that names the places he has gone awry.

The scenes of Affleck in the church are juxtaposed with powerful counterpoint scenes of Jackson in real confession. In a confession even more intimate than with a priest in a confessional, Jackson goes face-to-face with his ex-wife to name before her the places of sin in his life. He acknowledges how his decisions big and small have caused him to become the wrong person and caused their relationship to die. In this scene, meaning is found through honest confession, the kind of face-to-face confession that is found in a truly worshiping life.

Our prayers of confession call us to open ourselves to the intimacy and vulnerability of real confession. They poke us from our comfort zones and prickle our consciences. In these prayers, we name the places we have died, perhaps not even realizing the long slow death until the prayer names it for us. In confession we go face-to-face with ourselves, our neighbors, our God to say where we have died and caused death to others.

While there have been moments of recognition, those days when, like the cactus losing its skin, I finally realize my death, my sin most often is sin with the skin still on. It is the prickly sin that pierces and pokes those around me that I most often confess on a Sunday morning. It is the sin that needles and barbs my husband, my daughter, my driving, my living. It is the cold and prickly stuff of the day-to-day existence. It is the sin that keeps loved ones and strangers at arm's length instead of welcoming them in. It's not sin with ribs beheld bare, not deadened, but strangely alive, the sin that perks up in the wrong places and draws energy from the destructive. There is so much sin in the world this shouldn't just be a chapter on sin, but a book about sin. It would be as broad as our egos, as deep as our pockets, as wide as our appetites, and as high as our ambition. It would be a big book—but in no way could it ever possibly be as honest about the sin in our lives as it needed to be. Our sin is too dark, too repressed, too deadly even to be put into words.

It is Christ on the cross who combats our sin and calls us to a new confession—the confession of Christ himself. We turn in worship from confession of sin to the confession that Jesus Christ alone is Lord and Savior. The writer of Philippians describes this movement poetically as he prods us away from our sin and toward a confession of Christ as Lord: "Do nothing from selfish ambition or conceit, but in humility regard others as better than yourselves. Let each of you look not to your own interests, but to the interests of others. Let the same mind be in you that was in Christ Jesus . . . so that at the name of Jesus every knee should bend, in heaven and on earth and under the earth, and every tongue should confess that Jesus Christ is Lord" (Phil. 2:3–5, 10–11). Just as Sunday morning worship moves from our confession of sin to our confession of Jesus Christ as Lord and Savior, a worshiping life is constantly seeking to change lanes from our confession of sin to a confession of Christ as Lord that is made manifest in real ways in our day-to-day lives.

While we are constantly navigating between these two lanes, the cross stands as a clear road sign. So powerful is the cross's confession of Christ that it is only during the period of Eastertide that we do not even need to utter a prayer of confession. Christ has taken it upon himself. No Kyrie Eleison, no corporate prayers of confession, no calls to confession or times for silent reflection—at Easter we are called to confess Jesus Christ as Lord, and in place of the confession we offer prayers of adoration instead.

Those dead cactus in the desert, with skin stripped down and ribs bare, call me to a moment of confession to reflect on the sin and the places of death in my life. There are times when in a moment of grace, the dead cactus with its arms outstretched looks exactly like a cross. The ribs of the cactus fade and the image of the cross becomes clear. With arms outstretched, it embraces our confessions, hugs us in the midst of our prickliness, draws us in despite our sinful ways. In those moments I confess my sin and then I pray that my sin will recede and my life instead will become a clear witness to the cross in its confession of Christ alone as Lord and Savior.

Assurance of Pardon

"Simply accept the fact that you are accepted!"
If that happens to us, we experience grace.
After such an experience we may not be better than before,
And we may not believe more than before.
But everything is transformed.

— *Paul Tillich,*
"You Are Accepted"[1]

*R*eading these words from Paul Tillich's sermon, "You Are Accepted," one gets the feeling that Tillich wants to reach out from beyond the pulpit and beyond the page to grab the listeners and give them a little shaking. The italics are his. *"Simply accept the fact that you are accepted!"* In the sermon, he says it over and over again, in every paragraph, in a myriad of ways. He wants us to hear anew and be changed by the unbelievable fact that not only are we accepted, we are assured of God's pardon. Sin abounds, yes. But so much more so is the abounding, confounding, astounding grace of God.

It is unfortunate that in most services of worship the assurance of pardon is the most rote and ritualized element of all. Shrunk down to a two-line litany, it's easy to blink, yawn or daydream through the most pivotal point of the worship service. "In Jesus Christ, we are forgiven." Six words later it's over. How is it possible that everything is transformed in that moment? Yet we know the constraints of the time and place.

The assurance of pardon is the axis upon which all of worship revolves. We are left spinning without a center, caught up in the endless revolutions of sin and self unless we allow ourselves to be held together by this astounding axis. We come rolling into worship from all of our circles of life without God. Within minutes of our gathering, we are asked to name those places in our lives as individuals and as a corporate body that we need to confess. Thoughts spin to all of the sins of omission and sins of commission we have perpetrated throughout the week. Sixty seconds of confession? We could use an hour. Unison prayers written by somebody else? I have my own list to go by. Only one paragraph to express it all? I have pages to get off my chest. Give me a pen and paper so I might write a few letters of apology. Some confessions change dramatically from week to week; other sins are so engrained that the confession is always the same, and yet we always come back around to the same centering point, "In Jesus Christ, we are forgiven."

Once we have stopped spinning and have centered in, grabbing onto this axis for dear life, we are freed to hear the Word of God proclaimed and to offer in return our response to this good news. Worship revolves around our hearing and receiving these words of forgiveness. Yet why are these words so hard to receive? Tillich knew all our "buts" to this response: "But I'm not good enough." "But I'm still a sinner." "But God couldn't love someone like me."

At a youth conference last summer I met a sixteen-year-old boy, Peter, who had heard a lot of "buts" in his life. He knew the power and control that the word had over him. Having grown up in a home where acceptance didn't come easily, he struggled to feel good about himself. He was the most likable guy in the small group — funny and outgoing, handsome and warm. His charisma was both attractive and safe. Everyone felt comfortable around his easygoing, likable nature. Yet when he spoke about his family, his life, his self-doubts and fears, it was clear that he struggled with self-acceptance. Over the course of the week his ease in sharing helped the small group open up to safe sharing. At the end of the week, all in the group shared their highlights—their God moments—from the week. Many spoke of new friends, the small group, connections made in their own youth groups. Highlights were centered mostly in the development of relationships. A few spoke of moments in a worship service or keynote talk that challenged or transformed them. Peter's highlight stood out as wholly unique. "The highlight of my week? It was proclaiming God's glorious pardon to everybody at the outdoor worship service." While most would add "an assurance of," for Peter it was uniquely "God's glorious" pardon. While we might breeze through the assurance of pardon on any given Sunday morning, for Peter the highlight of his week was being able to say to a gathered crowd of senior high students, "You might feel worthless, you might feel like nobody cares, you might feel unaccepted, *but* . . ."

Perhaps one of the best words in the Bible is "but," along with "peace" and "love," "justice," and "mercy," even "God" or "Christ." One of the most gracious and awe-inspiring words upon which so much of scripture balances is this word "but." It's the word that grounds the Scripture seen on bumper stickers around the world— John 3:16: "God so loved the world that he gave his only Son, so that we should not perish but have eternal life." Over five thousand times in the NRSV this astounding word appears. "But" abounds in the Bible. In the Bible "but" isn't the basis for an excuse as we so often use the word in daily life. "But" is the foundation for receiving God's grace. As Psalm 86:15 says, "But you, O Lord, are a God merciful and gracious, slow to anger and abounding in steadfast love and faithfulness." "But" is an opposition to all of our enemies: "O Lord, how many are my foes. Many are rising against me, but you, O Lord, are a shield around me" (Ps. 3:3). "But" is the only thing that endures: "The grass withers, the flowers fade, but the word of our God will stand forever" (Isa. 40:7).

In the assurance of pardon, we announce God's glorious "but." Perhaps those will be the words that grab our attention in worship. The assurance of pardon is the axis upon which all of worship, all of life, revolves. Tillich recognizes that "but" by saying, "We may not be better than before . . . but everything is transformed." With a sure and hearty acceptance of God's pardon, all of life is held together centered in God's grace and mercy. And this, according to Peter, is glorious.

Years ago I heard an activist in education reform recall his early days of teaching after graduation from a prestigious university. His parents thought he was crazy to accept a postgraduation position teaching in the public school system of South Boston. Why pay for a top-notch education to accept such a low-paying, meaningless job?

His parents were unsupportive, and for a time, uncommunicative. In the meantime, the young teacher struggled through the school system. Eager to empower and excite the imagination, he drew on the poetry of Langston Hughes. The administration of the school, angered by his dismissal of the accepted curriculum and threatened by his empowerment of the students, fired him. The firing caused an uproar in the community. Teachers, parents, students and members of the community marched in protest toward the city hall. The young teacher, embarrassed by the publicity, wanted to stay home that day. Arriving late he saw the parade of people marching toward the town center. What he didn't expect to see were the two people leading the parade, carrying a banner in support of him—his parents, thereby shouting out their pardon of his actions, showing their love for their son. One might say that the pardon is held up as a banner over our worship and lives.

God's banner over us is as bold as these words, "For God so loved the world that he gave his only Son, so that we might not perish *but* have eternal life." In worship, how can we depict the magnitude of these words? How can we honor their glorious telling of Christ's death for our sins without scaling it down to a six-word size? The assurance of pardon is the axis upon which all of worship holds, it is glorious in its telling of Christ's sacrifice for our sins; it is a banner in boldly proclaiming God's acceptance of us no matter what. Because of these very things, it forms the praxis of our ministry. Because we are pardoned, we must pardon others, forgiving debts, forgoing hurts, forbidding retaliation. God is for us and so in turn we are for others. In that moment, everything is transformed. We may be sinners, but God's banner over us is love.

Proclaiming

Proclaiming

I am large; I contain multitudes.
                    —*Walt Whitman, "Song of Myself"*[1]

On the corner of 29th and Wharton streets in central Philadelphia, a bold vision of peace is artfully proclaimed. Anyone who knows Philadelphia knows that the corner of 29th and Wharton is an unlikely place for peace to exist. Known to residents as Gray's Ferry, the area has long been troubled by racial tension. White flight in the 1960s, riots born of economic collapse in the 1970s, competitive backlash of a white basketball team against several black basketball teams in the 1980s all led to national attention in the 1990s when a teenager was shot after escalating violence. As one resident said, "You learned quickly around here where you belonged, and where you didn't."[2]

It was precisely in the midst of this troubled area that the founders of the Mural Arts Program of Philadelphia envisioned a bold proclamation of peace. The Mural Arts Program was developed in 1984 as an antigraffiti effort. After spending hundreds of thousands of dollars each year repainting city walls, a few concerned citizens pictured walls covered not with graffiti but with murals, and youth not serving time in detention centers but time as artists. The folks of the Mural Arts Program (M.A.P.) had a new map for the city, one laid out with new visions for a community once known only for violence and decay. Within a few years, the graffiti problem had been turned around and Philadelphia was quickly becoming known as "the mural capital of the United States." Thousands of murals enlivened street corners once known only for gang violence, drug sales and murder. Hundreds of people called with offers to paint the walls on their homes or in their neighborhoods with a new vision. Once a wall was chosen, volunteers from the Mural Arts Program would work with the community to discern a new vision for their neighborhood to be proclaimed through a mural.

Even with this history of success, coming up with a consensus for the corner of 29th and Wharton proved to be problematic. Community members thought the money could be better spent; others thought the idea was hypocritical; some felt as if a mural of unity would be imposed on them. Others thought the mural would simply be a reminder of the problems that continued to plague their community.

Community members of all beliefs gathered to discuss the potential project. They talked about the tragedies that had marked their community. From there, they began a process to determine a vision for peace in the community. After many proposals, one stood out among all others: eleven hands laid one upon another, five black, six white, and these words: "Blessed are the peacemakers; for they shall be called the children of God." It was clear that this was the consensus of the community.

After choosing eleven hands and sketching a preliminary drawing, the artists got to work. Carefully charting out every crease and wrinkle in each hand, the artists laid out the vision. But the vision proclaimed was more than eleven hands and a verse from the Bible projected onto a city wall. The vision proclaimed spoke multitudes as black artists and white artists worked side by side, night after night, for six weeks. Each evening, when residents used to shut themselves safely in their homes to avoid any violence, they instead came out to watch and share snacks. Children from the community volunteered to help and even began painting other walls in the surrounding area. Here the "Peace Wall" was born.

Those charged with getting into the pulpit each Sunday know that they face a similar challenge. A mural is to be painted—one that honors suffering, claims the heart of the community and boldly paints a new vision. Any preacher who has taken a homiletics class has heard the professor say, "Every person out there in the pew has a broken heart. How are you going to preach to him and her?" So many tragedies told and untold sit in the pew that any preacher wonders upon occasion two things: "Who am I that I should proclaim the good news?" and "Even given the gospel message, what shall I say to them?"

These were the first questions on the mind of Moses when he encountered the Holy One of Israel at Horeb (Exodus 3). The most indescribable of murals was painted before him out of the simplest of elements—flames of fire and an unconsumed bush. The largeness of God was proclaimed in that moment—God's presence, "Here I am"; God's past, "I am the God of your father, the God of Abraham, the God of Isaac, and the God of Jacob"; and God's future yet to be proclaimed, "I have observed the misery of my people. . . . So come, I will send you to Pharaoh to bring my people, the Israelites, out of Egypt."

In that all-encompassing moment, Moses trembled and balked. "Who am I that I should go to Pharaoh, and bring the Israelites out of Egypt? . . . If I come to the Israelites and say to them, 'The God of your ancestors has sent me to you,' and they ask me, 'What is his name?' what shall I say to them?"

In response to these huge questions of proclamation and the most basic of human instincts, to recoil, God offered the most perplexing and profound answer: "I AM WHO I AM." God responded with a play on the verb "to be," and with that the Holy One of Israel sent Hebrew scholars to scratch their heads and turn some pages. Certainly this Holy One of Israel was having some fun being punny, but so also was Yahweh offering the most basic of truths. When asked, "What shall I proclaim?" God answers, "I have been there, I am there, and I will be there." Rolling all senses of the verb "to be" into one enigmatic phrase, God puns on God's own divine name "Yahweh." With that, Yahweh calls on Moses and his listeners to remember all of the "I ams" in which God has revealed God's very self until this point. "I am the God of Abraham, the God of Isaac and the God of Jacob" is only a small fraction of the story. This Holy One of Israel is the God of Dinah and Sarah, of Hagar and Tamar, God of the ark and the idol, God of Leah and Rachel. This Holy One of Israel could very well utter, "I am chaos and creation. I am darkness, I am light. I am a ladder and a stone. I am food and I am famine." These names and images evoke the very presence of Yahweh. "I am what I am," Yahweh says to Moses. In so doing God sparks our imagination to consider the multitude of possibilities.

For those who need help considering the multitude of possibilities God intended in the utterance of the divine name, Christ comes along with a paintbrush in hand. The multitude of possibilities are condensed into seven images, but the possibilities within those seven images for our imagination and our spiritual nourishment are endless. "I am the bread of life" (John 6:35); "I am the light of the world" (8:12); "I am the gate for the sheep" (10:7); "I am the good shepherd" (10:11); "I am the resurrection and the life" (11:25); "I am the way and the truth and the life" (14:6); "I am the true vine" (15:1).

Standing on any street corner in the United States, the mural Christ paints of the true vine is a vivid reminder that so many other things call us to tap into them for nourishment. On any decrepit wall that needs rebuilding, "I am the light of the world" speaks volumes. For any community that needs to work through a process of understanding and reconciliation, "I am the good shepherd" is the picture to paint. These seven "I am" statements develop our understanding of the true nature of Christ. A solid Christology could be formed just from these seven statements. Yet they do so much more than show the true nature of Christ; they open our imagination and they tap into that deep part of ourselves that is hungry and thirsty for more than words. These images paint pictures of Christ all around us.

A group of scholars led by Sharon Daloz Parks interviewed one hundred young adults working to make a difference for the common good. Parks wanted to know what sparks within these young people ignited that fire for fighting. What had gotten them past the balking that Moses began with? Comparing the one hundred interviewed, Parks and her colleagues determined that the answer was deceptively simple. The young adults shared three things in common. First, each had a strong sense of self-identity. They all knew clearly their gifts and their weaknesses. Second, each had a strong vision for what the world should be like and the barriers inherent in the institutional structures that prevented that vision from becoming reality. The third characteristic this group shared was surprising, Parks and her colleagues noted that each of the individuals referred to a symbol or image, something beyond themselves and somewhat transcendent in nature, that guided them in their thinking.[3] A burning bush unconsumed by fire, hands clasped on a mural unconsumed by violence or graffiti, and a

vision of creation unconsumed by chaos are all examples of proclamation that stimulate the imagination and challenge the individual to
design bold new ways of taking that vision to new places and to people in need.

Preacher and layperson alike are challenged to paint the gospel
message. Standing on our street corners, looking around at a world in
need, we grapple with what tools to use and what message to proclaim.
Our paintbrushes are held in the minds of those who hear our words
and see our actions. With a dapple and a brushstroke, a picture is
painted whether we intend to do so or not. The paid staff of the Mural
Arts Program struggle with the same issue. Once the community
decides the vision for the mural, one of the paid staff members designs
a preliminary drawing that becomes the basis for the mural. But then
the mural is turned back to the community, where volunteers, includ-
ing children and former graffiti artists, pick up their brushes and begin
to work side by side with the professional staff. The mural becomes a
collaborative effort. So too does preaching. For any artist or preacher
intent on perfection, the ideal becomes an elusive goal. But for those
open to the kind of perfection that the Holy Spirit brings through col-
laboration in community, then a truly perfect proclamation can be
offered. Fred Rogers writes, "The space between [the preacher] and
the needy listener is holy ground. The Holy Spirit uses that space in
marvelously, wonderful ways."[4] I see that space as a blank canvas.

My favorite mural in Philadelphia was recently demolished at the
corner of 40th Street and Powelton Avenue to make room for new
construction. The famous artist Sidney Goodman collaborated with
the program and other volunteers to paint "Boy with Raised Arm." In
the mural a young African American boy stands against a dark back-
ground. With decrepit walls shadowed behind him, he gracefully
raises one arm with a clenched fist. The mural conveys the need of
this young boy to be just a tad bit taller, just a little larger than he is.
This was all the mural contained, and then the Holy Spirit moved
along that canvas and words from a Walt Whitman poem were added.
"I am large," the mural proclaims for the boy and all others who need
the same encouragement. "I contain multitudes."

Those of us in the pew and the pulpit need the same enlargement.
"I am large," Yahweh says in a way to Moses as God utters the divine

name. "I contain multitudes." "I am large," Christ claims when he says, "I am the bread of life." If you think you've heard it proclaimed before, listen again. "I am large enough to feed five thousand with just five loaves of bread and two fish." "I am large enough for billions of people over the centuries to keep picking up those crumbs of bread and doing this in remembrance of me." "I am large enough to feed the hungry in body and in spirit." The Spirit whispers, "Before me lies a blank canvas. You may say one word, but through me people will hear that word in multitudes of ways."

Jane Kenyon refers to the multitudes the Trinity can proclaim in her poem, "Briefly It Enters, and Briefly Speaks."

> I am the maker, the lover, and the keeper . . .
>
> When the young girl who starves
> sits down to a table
> she will sit beside me . . .
>
> I am food on the prisoner's plate.[5]

These words enlarge for us a God who makes the world, a Christ who loves the world, and the Spirit that keeps the world, while at the same time framing for us particular ways of seeing the Trinity at work among us. She paints a picture of maker, lover and keeper. She paints a picture of bread on a plate. For those who would dismiss her interpretation of the Trinity as a reduction to functionality, much is lost. Kenyon gives fresh words to the gospel and a new picture of how we might see it at work in the world.

The challenge to preachers is to place food on the plate. We face critical yet hungry ears. We hope to enlarge the kingdom, but also to frame barriers and problems. We try to get people to pause briefly in the places and situations that desperately need more than a moment's notice. How can we paint over and over again new pictures that proclaim the maker, the lover and the keeper who is at work as the Trinity among us and through us and beside us? How can we set out that loaf of homemade bread that will feed the hungry?

In the movie *Wit*, Emma Thompson plays Vivian Bearing, a professor of English, dying of cancer. Academia has been her life's ambition; she has lost friendships and family in pursuit of achievement.

Now, as her life comes to a close, she is surrounded not by books, students, papers or journal articles, but by the lonely walls of a hospital room. The movie is almost a one-woman show as it chronicles her personal battle with the worst of evils. Our pain for her grows as her loneliness increases. One nurse befriends her. Though caught between the demands she faces in her job, the nurse slows down to be with Vivian. One day she pulls out hand lotion and gives Vivian a hand massage. Another day she offers a popsicle to share. "I am bread on a prisoner's plate," Kenyon offers, and the movie begs to add, "I am a popsicle shared." The sharing becomes pure sacrament.

Near the end of the movie, a mentor tracks Vivian down. She offers a reading first of the poetry of John Donne. At any other point in life this would have been a divine offering. But here Vivian dismisses it for simple closeness with her friend. The mentor calls out her name and climbs into the hospital bed. "Let me read you a story then," she offers. So begins the reading of *The Runaway Bunny:* "Once there was a little bunny who wanted to run away. So he said to his mother, 'I am running away.' 'If you run away,' said his mother, 'I will run after you. For you are my little bunny.'"

So begins the gospel truth. Her proclamation is as gentle as the touch of their bodies in the bed, as genuine as the simple utterance of Vivian's name and as truth-filled as the story told. I am what I am. I am the runaway bunny. I am her mother. I am the questions the toddler asks endlessly. I am the bush unconsumed by fire. I am a sermon preached not perfectly, but with ears open to hearing and the spirit ready to intervene. I am the sacred ground between pulpit and listener. I am canvas and paintbrush. I am the maker. I am the lover. I am the keeper. I am a mural painted on a street corner, eleven hands clasped. I am a hand massage. I am a popsicle. I am a children's story read aloud. I am touch and taste. I am food on the prisoner's plate. I am the bread of life. I am large. I contain multitudes. I am proclaimed in all of these things and so much more.

Prayer for Illumination

The hen flings a single pebble aside
with her yellow, reptilian foot.
Never in eternity the same sound—
a small stone falling on a red leaf.

The juncture of twig and branch,
scarred with lichen, is a gate
we might enter, singing.

Things: simply lasting, then
failing to last: water, a blue heron's
eye, and the light passing
between them: into light all things
must fall, glad at last to have fallen.
                    —Jane Kenyon, "Things"[1]

A poet's day is a constant prayer for illumination, observing daily life incessantly, taking note of the small details that illumine and inspire. Some days are dark. Some days are dull. Some days no poems call out. Then, when a hen flings a single pebble, the recognition that this sound will never again be repeated inspires a poem. The poet knows the arduous task of waiting and looking thousands of days and ways for that cast of light passing to illumine the blue heron, the twig and the branch, the yellow reptilian foot. Poet Naomi Shihab Nye calls these moments of illumination "the gleam of particulars."

We look for the gleam of particulars in this world God created because we cannot manufacture that gleam of light ourselves. We like to think we can. With the advent of industrial light, with the turning of the clock for daylight savings time, with the glow of neon advertising things to claim our souls, we believe we can manufacture light and its powerful glow. The irony of this day and age is that there are so many things flashing at us, it makes finding true light an even more difficult task.

James Turrell, a Quaker, is so angered by the overabundance of manufactured light in our culture that he has dedicated his career as an artist to getting his viewers to experience light in a new way. Inspired by the Quaker prayer spoken on the way to a gathering, "Go inside and greet the light," he invites his viewers to do the same as they enter a museum housing his creations. Rothko-like canvases apparent to the viewer's eyes are facades created by the cast of light. One of his works, an entire room, pitch black, is an invitation for the viewer to sit—twenty minutes or more to achieve the effect of a glimmer of light that comes in the midst of the darkness. The wait in the dark makes the viewer uncomfortable. Sit in the dark with strangers? No thank you. Devote twenty minutes of my lunch hour at the museum squeezed into an already-too-busy day to wait for light to dawn? I'll walk on to the next exhibit. We don't have the patience to look for illumination that brightens not by the glow of a lamp but by the effort of truly looking to see.

If we don't have the twenty minutes of patience needed to see this light in a museum exhibit, how then can we sit through Scripture and a sermon and wait for illumination? Thorny texts, dry preaching, a baby's cry. We don't have the patience or desire to sit and wait. With a dark world at our fingertips, we want the flick of a switch to make it brighter. Who can wait for someone to ignite a real fire?

In the desert, there is a plant that blooms fiery sparks of red. This fire occurs at the tips of one of the most lifeless plants in the desert, the ocotillo. Most of the year the ocotillo looks hopeless, like a spray of sticks and thorns. Standing six feet tall or higher, the plant consists of ten to twenty long sticks gathered at its base, spread open at the ends of the branches. It doesn't have the kitschiness of a cactus, or the personality of a prickly pear. It looks dead, lifeless and downright dismal most days of the year. Then the winter snowmelt brings just enough hydration and the spring sun brings just enough light to call the ocotillo out of death and into life. Slowly small leaves creep up its branches and then ignite at the top into a fiery red glow of feathery flowers. These red flowers guide the hummingbirds on their spring trek north.

Sometimes what we see in our lives or in the Scripture texts for the day looks a lot like those sticks and thorns. As one congregation member asked upon hearing the Scripture one Sunday, "I came to church to hear this?" We don't want to hear about the thorny side of judgment or the sticky texts of terror. The fire that ignites isn't the passion within us to hear and to serve, but the fiery anger of the truth of being known. So scared are we of hearing and knowing, we retreat. We aren't willing to put ourselves into the darkness of a Scripture text because its shadows can at times be more apparent than its light. We don't have the patience to wait for the fiery flowers to bloom.

The Guggenheim Museum in New York City offered a retrospective show of the paintings of Robert Rauschenberg. Known for their immense and colorful collages, one painting stood out as entirely different. It was one of those paintings that begs the complaint "I could have painted that!" Yet its simplicity was deceptive. Painted entirely black, it had a single slice of light piercing the center of the canvas. The title of the painting didn't give much hint to its meaning: *Untitled*. But then, an apparent afterthought, there in parentheses was another thought almost scribbled in. *Untitled (Nightblooming)* was the title in its entirety. Was the night blooming into further darkness overtaking the light? Or was the night slowly blooming and unfolding into light?

This is the question the church faces each week as the pastor and congregation stand before the dark canvas of the world with the small sliver of illumination held between the covers of our Bible. We pray for illumination that the words of Scripture might unfold and bloom, light into light, light out of darkness, dead sticks into fiery flowers so that all the world might witness the glory of God. Darkness will not have the last word. Night will not bloom even darker and deeper into night. Christ pierces the darkness. His life stands like a small sliver against the dark canvas of injustice, against the inability to accept God's grace revealed. Through his life, light overtakes the darkness.

Recently the Catholic Church realized it had not fully emphasized the light shed into the world by the life of Christ. Its rosary prayers consisted of the joyful mysteries of the annunciation, the sorrowful mysteries of the passion and the glorious mysteries of the resurrection. But what about his healing and teaching? What about the light cast at the table of the Eucharist and the glow of the transfiguration? In an effort to illuminate even more fully the life of Christ, the church added "the luminous mysteries" of Christ's life—his baptism, the wedding at Cana, his proclamation in parables, the transfiguration and the Eucharist.

These luminous mysteries reveal another artist at work painting streaks of light across the dark canvas of the world. We pray for illumination that we might see this hand at work. As I walk through the desert, my prayer, like the poet's, is to see something new, that some wildflower, creature, stone or mountain might be illumined in a new light, in a new way.

We don't just go inside to greet the light; we go outside to the everyday street corners to look for illumination. In the movie *Smoke*, the owner of a Brooklyn tobacco shop, Auggie Wren, prays for illumination by taking a single photograph each day. You would think that the subject of the photograph would be different each day, but he takes a picture of the same street corner every day at the same time, 8 a.m. One day a customer notices the camera and asks about it. Auggie pulls out his photograph album filled with four thousand pictures of the same street corner. The customer, seemingly surprised, shrugs and Auggie responds, "This is my life's work. It's my corner. A record of my little spot in the world. But things happen here too." The customer begins flipping through the pictures quickly and Auggie retorts, "Slow down. You'll never get it unless you slow down, my friend." The customer does, but he still doesn't get it. "They're all the same," he dismisses. Auggie explains further, "But each one is different . . . there is summer light and autumn light. Each day the light hits the earth at a different angle." Finally, as the customer looks closely at the pictures, he notices the change of lights and shadows, cars and passersby, that illumine this corner of the world. In the midst of a smoky tobacco shop, a too-busy consumer is taught to pray for illumination to see the light amid the haze of life.

Last year the citizens of Tucson were thrilled to have the opportunity to greet the light as a meteor shower promised dazzle in the middle of the night. My decision whether to set my alarm clock for 3 a.m. to witness it became a spiritual struggle. I wanted to see the shower, but sleep was tempting. I succumbed to temptation and missed the meteor shower, which occurs less than once a century. The following Sunday, one pastor shared in sermon about setting the alarm and waking up his children. Setting their alarm clock became a prayer for illumination. The world is dark, but the night is blooming into light. Our challenge is to pray for the illumination that will help us see it.

Children's Sermon

Truly I tell you, whoever does not receive the kingdom of God as a little child will never enter it.
—*Luke 18:17*

I've had an ongoing reception problem. When I moved to Tucson a few years ago, I was unable to find the perfect radio station. A radio station is important. It helps set the mood for the day, brings you up-to-date news, and provides the necessary tunes as a soundtrack for the trek about town. My inability to find the perfect radio station matched my inability to feel settled after a major cross-country move. Each time I got in my car, I'd desperately scan the channels hoping to find one that would connect. Nothing did. Longing for the familiarity of the old stations, I finally gave up and stopped looking. Several weeks later I was talking to a friend as I got into the car. "Did you realize your antenna is down?" she asked me. No wonder I had reception problems! Raising the antenna brought not only a whole new span of music and news, but also an awareness of how easy it is to drive around with the antenna down.

At other times in my life I have had reception problems—change after change after change has been difficult to receive. Situations played out in my life and the lives of those I love that have been difficult to receive. Even harder are the reception problems that come in hearing the gospel. Receiving forgiveness? At times a problem. Receiving the stranger and the foreigner and the enemy as a loved one? Definitely a reception problem at times. Receiving the truth and the wonder and the goodness of Christ? I wonder if my antenna is up.

Christ knows the problem we have with reception. Even though he tells parables and truths with points as sharp as any antenna, we often don't get the message. Here in Luke 18:17 he speaks over the static saying, "Truly I tell you, whoever does not receive the kingdom of God as a little child will never enter it." God knows that children know how to receive. Children know how to receive truth that we adults are sadly no longer open to.

Children are much more receptive. Their antennas are up. They are tuned in and ready to grasp the world at their fingertips. We adults don't always get it. The gospel reminds us that children are much better at reception, particularly when it comes to the kingdom of God— they get it. Why then do we presume to give sermons to children? Why don't we have the children give the sermon to us? I have heard a lot of bad children's sermons. I have given even worse. I've talked at them, around them, above them.

It is difficult to tune ourselves to exactly their channel. A project entitled "Narratives from the Crib" examined how adults talk down to children. The project began inadvertently in the home of two college professors who noticed their daughter Emily talking herself to sleep each night. They started recording both the conversations they had with her as well as the conversations she had with herself. What they learned was that Emily spoke to herself in a much more advanced fashion than they, her parents, communicated. One of the scholars who listened to the tapes wrote, "In general, her speech to herself is so much richer and more complex [than her speech to adults]. . . . Once the lights are out and her parents leave the room, Emily reveals a stunning mastery of language forms we would never have suspected from her [everyday] speech."[1] When we consider the effects of such communication theologically, then it becomes clear that in our not giving children the credit of being able to speak beyond their years, we might miss the very voice of God in our midst.

If we turn the dial to the other side, we err on speaking over their heads. Words intended for good become too abstract, too disconnected, too removed from their frame of reference. A group of ophthalmologists asked Mister Rogers to help them speak to children.

Children were coming into their offices scared and concerned that once they closed their eyes for a checkup, their eyes might never open again. He agreed to write a chapter for a book that would help them calm such frightened children. Mister Rogers had one of his assistants do a first draft of the book, and when she brought it to him for review, Mister Rogers crossed out the entire chapter and wrote the following, "You were a child once, too." From there she rewrote the chapter.[2]

Children's sermons call us to a new level of receptivity: first, to receive the fact that children have knowledge and the ability to communicate that surpass their years and our understanding; second, to receive the fact that yes, we were children once too. Erring too much on either side can have undue effects not just in our worship, but also in life when we miss what children are saying to us. Their reception is without parallel, and their communication speaks of God. Their words and actions make excellent children's sermons; as we listen to them we find it easier to tune into their channel.

John Michael was the first to tell me a children's sermon. He was about four when he went out one day into his backyard to play. The challenge of his day was to start a bug collection. The find was discovering a cocoon draped in a corner of his back porch. He was outside for hours, much longer than usual. At times when we checked on him, we saw him in his galoshes stomping and jumping in apparent impatience. When he finally came inside and collapsed on the sofa, frustration was smeared across his face. "I've been trying and trying," he told his mom, "but I just couldn't get the butterfly out." It wasn't a three-point sermon, nor could it be summed up in a clever acronym. It wasn't twenty minutes; it wasn't even conclusive in its message. But a sermon it was—a sermon about patience and timing and waiting for God and our stomping impatiently in the midst of that waiting. I've thought a lot about that sermon.

John Michael also gave a great funeral sermon. His elderly neighbor Dottie died from cancer. Dottie and John Michael had enjoyed many days together—bug collecting, painting, reading and making music together in her living room. Shortly after Dottie died, her son came to stay at John Michael's house for a few days. Grief was still heavy and palpable for all. The morning after the funeral everyone sat down to grits and eggs. John Michael, just four, looked across the table and declared, "I talked to Dottie last night." "You did?" his mother asked. "Yeah, I dreamt about her hanging out with the angels. She looked at me and told me she was alright and I didn't need to worry about her anymore." It was in those words so clearly stated by John Michael that a sermon was offered that morning. When a four-year-old says, "She told me she was alright and I saw that she was with the angels," what more could we possibly add to that message of hope? How could we doubt that in God's kingdom Dottie is there alongside the angels?

I have heard many a children's sermon preached from the mouths of toddlers and teens. "The kingdom of God is perfection in all seasons," fourteen-year-old Adrian preached. "In the kingdom of God there is no time to feel unimportant," Patty, just fifteen, sums up in response to Ecclesiastes 3. "The popular thing isn't always the right thing, and the right thing isn't always popular," proclaims thirteen-year-old Mark after discussing Romans 12:1–2. Who needs a three-point sermon? Let's listen to the focused points, antenna-like, of these kids.

It is Anthony's sermon on the kingdom of God that haunts me, though. I learned of Anthony in Johnathan Kozol's book *Amazing Grace*. Anthony knew loss and suffering. A single mother in the Bronx was raising him. He had just lost a young uncle in a gang-related shooting. Yet Anthony was resilient. He loved Edgar Alan Poe and his poetry. When Anthony first met Kozol, they spoke about their favorite poem, "The Raven," and its famous word, "nevermore." They discussed the meaning of the short story "The Mask of the Red Death," and what it meant for those who were not able to face suffering and living in the midst of a broken world. Kozol, wanting to learn more from Anthony, asked him to write an assignment on what the kingdom of God might look like.

Weeks later, Anthony turned in this challenge written on college-ruled paper and carefully handprinted:

> No violence will there be in heaven, no guns or drugs or IRS. If you still feel lonely in your heart, or bitterness, you'll know that you are not there. As for television, forget it! No one will look at you from the outside. People will see you from the inside. All the people from the street will be there. You'll recognize all the chil-

dren who have died when they were little. God will be there. He'll be happy that we have arrived.[3]

On the top of the sheet Anthony had scrawled, "CHECK OUT THE BACK!" When Kozol turned the page over he saw a drawing of a raven with the word emerging from its mouth, "Nevermore." At first Kozol didn't get it. "Nevermore?" In typical adult fashion, for him it didn't totally add up at first. Not until Kozol attended the funeral of Anthony's uncle did it make sense. At the funeral, Anthony read the Scripture passage taken from Revelation 21 and given special emphasis by Anthony: "And on that day there will be a new heaven and a new earth. Nevermore will there be any suffering. Nevermore will there be any pain. Nevermore will there be any tears. But God will wipe away what tears are left from their eyes."

Even Leah, my infant daughter, receives the kingdom of God so much more openly than I do. And she preaches wonderful sermons about it, without using any words. Sometimes her sermon is laughter; other days it is a lesson of discovery and wonder. There are sermons on prayer and sermons on play that are some of her favorite ones to preach. My favorite sermon is her one on sharing. After devouring some of the snack of the day, she'll offer up a bite for me. Without any words she lets me know, as she raises her pudgy hand to my mouth with mushy peach in hand, "Mom, you've nourished me. I've happily received it. I want you to have a taste. Will you receive it?"

Old Testament Lesson

Let the words of my mouth and the meditation of my heart
be acceptable to you, O Lord,
my rock and my redeemer.

—Psalm 19:14

*E*very time I hear this passage from the Psalms, often offered as a prayer of the pastor before a sermon, I experience both a connect and a disconnect. "My rock and my redeemer" are words that speak to me at a very deep level of God. The way I connect isn't literal; it's much more of an internal response—this is the God that I know. The disconnect comes through the odd pairing of words. "My rock and my redeemer" seem like two different kinds of entities, almost at odds with one another. A noun that is solid and fortifying and carries with it no action is paired with another noun that speaks of a process. The rock is impenetrable and immovable, while the redeemer penetrates my soul to bring about salvation and moves me to a new way of living.

In the Old Testament, Jacob first calls God a rock as he passes on a blessing to his sons before his death. When he speaks of Joseph, Jacob offers these words: "Yet his bow remained taut and his arms were made agile . . . by the name of the Shepherd, the Rock of Israel" (Gen. 49:24). From that point on, the image of God as a rock is abundant. God is a rock of refuge, a fortifying rock, the rock of our salvation. The Old Testament writers put forth this image that carries with it strength and fortitude to describe the Lord our God. God is the foundation, the fortress, the refuge. Immovable and unchangeable are attributes implied within this metaphor. Although in speaking of God as a rock there is a danger that the metaphor will become too abstract, too impersonal, too naturalistic, there is a richness that overcomes the danger. God draws the feet of the psalmist "up from the desolate pit, out of the miry bog, and sets [his] feet upon a rock, making [his] steps secure" (Ps. 40:2), and with his renewed foundation comes our salvation as well. The psalmist recognizes as well that no other god compares: "For who is God except the Lord? And who is a rock besides our God?" (Ps. 18:31). Certainly there is no other who can live up to this name.

"Trust in the Lord forever," says the prophet Isaiah, "for in the Lord God you have an everlasting rock" (Isa. 26:4). "O Lord, my rock and my redeemer," soothes the psalmist (Ps. 19:14). The image of God as a rock is one that sturdies our convictions in God as a shelter, a refuge, a stability. John and Katherine Paterson, in their book *Images of God*, explain it this way:

> In a landscape where there are hardly any trees, a great boulder can be seen from a long distance away. It may provide the only shade for miles, and it seems strong and immovable. Rock serves as the foundation for building and for protection from enemies. Over and over again in the Bible, rock stands for dependability and shelter.[1]

The image of God as a rock took on new meaning when my husband and I visited the Hayden Planetarium in New York City. One humongous rock anchored the corner of the Earth Room. Turning the corner to get a better view my husband said, "This is one time I am sure of my calling. Just imagine, there are people who make a living by studying rocks like this one." No sooner had he said it when we saw a man, magnifying glass in hand, pressed up against the rock. We laughed at the coincidence of word and sight.

Throughout the day we were stimulated by shows and stars, words and wonderings, but it was the man studying the rock that remained on my mind. With magnifying glass in hand, eyes pressed against the lines of the rock, he was reading a story. So much of what we know about how the world was created, creatures that lived before us, civilizations that have come and gone, the universe beyond us—so much of these stories, our stories—are preserved and told in rocks like this one. I realized in seeing the man reading the rock that God, the rock of our mothers and our fathers, tells a story as well. There was a history present in this rock told through lines and layers and fossils. Time and pressure had formed this rock, and the effects of these elements could be told through the story lines.

In the movie *Shawshank Redemption*, Tim Robbins plays Andy, a man wrongly convicted of murder. He serves years before he finally manages an escape by carving a tunnel out of his room into the recesses of the prison building that would eventually lead him out through the sewer. Every night he dug at the walls, covering the hole with a poster. When the hole grew large enough, he was able to climb in each night and continue digging behind the poster. Each morning, he filled his pockets with the dirt from his digging and released it through the holes in his pockets as he walked around the yard. He carved some of the rocks he dug out, making intricate chess sets and statues. His pieces were prized among the inmates. Once Andy had escaped, his friends began to draw together the story of his daring escape. When one realized what Andy had done with the rocks, he explained, "Andy knew about rocks. Just as rocks are formed by time and pressure, so was Andy. Prison is all about time and pressure."

God's story is told within this earthen rock through its very layers and lines and fossils that are shaped through time and pressure. God shapes these at times corrosive elements into the very story of our salvation. These lines tell the story of God the Father of Abraham, Isaac and Jacob. Their very names tell their stories. Abraham, "the father of a multitude," tells the story of someone who doubted over and over again God's promise for his life. Taking matters into his own hands he seemed to put everything at risk, even his own wife and son. Yet from his seed, even at a very old age, the impossible happened. A multitude was born that lasts until this day, not just among Christians but for Jews and Muslims alike. His story line tells multitudes about God's promises. Isaac, "laughter," draws a smile from all who know the circumstances of his birth. What did his friends think when they met his wizened mother and father? How did he explain the age of his parents? Sarah, his mother, laughed in the presence of angels when it was announced she would give birth way after her child-bearing years. His story line gives us permission to laugh in hope with the angels at the improbable promises of God. They can come true. Then Jacob, who entered the world grasping the heel of his twin brother, Esau—his story to me is a lifetime of grasping—grasping for the birthright that was truly his brother's, grasping his father's blessing while breaking his relationship with Esau, grasping for forgiveness and reconciliation, grasping in the night to win a wrestling match with a divine presence, grasping in the midst of his own brokenness for a relationship with God through worship. His name means both "heel-grabber" and "supplanter," and his story line gives witness to both. We know the ways he grabs and grasps, yet we also know the way that God supplants both tendencies within us. These are just the beginning of the story lines. Within these stories are the stories of Sarah and Hagar, Ishmael and Esau, Rachel and Leah. Running our fingers over these lines, we read ourselves in these stories.

When we trace our fingers over those lines, we read the story of a genealogical line that used surprising, seemingly unredeemable people to give birth to Jesus Christ. Bridging the gap from Old Testament to New, the Gospel of Matthew begins with the lines of a family tree drawn for all to see: "An account of the genealogy of Jesus the Messiah, the son of David, the son of Abraham" (Matt. 1:1). From there Matthew goes on to develop the generations beyond Abraham, Isaac and Jacob, to include the stories of David and Solomon, Boaz and Ruth, Tamar and Rahab. This genealogy gives witness to battle lines fought and overcome, prophetic visions laid out like a plumb line, lines that are saved as a remnant is preserved. The lines of this genealogy are by no means straight; they break and crack under the pressures of being human, and yet the line is maintained. These lines are preserved for all time within the story of God as our rock.

The lines give guidance for living as laws are made and ordinances decreed. These lines frame the boundaries for our living as God's people. We follow the commands of the Ten Commandments, walk in the way of the Sabbath, proclaim years of Jubilee and offer up the first-fruits of our labor. Lines are laid out for a form of worship that is not sensory experience or ritualized action, but one lived out by doing justice, sharing bread, clothing the naked and letting the oppressed go free. These are the lines we live by. They are contained in the very being of God, our rock. Through these boundaries a people are called, a community created, a way of living fashioned.

These are the lines laid out in the Old Testament through the Writings, the Prophets, and the books of the Law. Yet as we read these ancient lines, stories of violence and suffering emerge. Ask any person about the Old Testament and you might hear a response like this: "I've never really liked the Old Testament"; "It's too hard to read"; "God seems to be a violent God, a different God, than the one I know from the New Testament." There is good reason for these statements. Encrusted into the very presence of God our rock are these fossils that tell of rape, torture, violence and inexcusable human sin. Babies are sacrificed, women are brutally murdered, other nations suffer as the promised land is fought for and achieved.

I received my very first Bible when I was nine in my fourth grade Sunday school class. It was a *Good News for Modern Man Bible.* The day we were presented with them, we spent the morning making them our own. We covered them with felt and used pipe cleaners to make a design with our names on the front. I remember the eagerness I felt to begin reading. I was fascinated that I could open up midway and turn right to the Psalms. I am not sure if it was on the first day of our receiving the Bibles, or shortly after, that we read the story of Sodom and Gomorrah. I shuddered as I read about fire and ashes and felt guilty when I realized I would have most likely turned to a pillar of salt like Lot's wife. To this day I remember the visceral feeling I internalized upon reading this story. Who is this God that destroys cities and punishes a woman for expressing grief?

Just when we begin to feel embedded in the questions that arise from some of these fossilized stories, we remember the second half of the phrase "O Lord, my rock and my redeemer." Even with the violence and suffering present in some of the Old Testament stories, people still bowed down to worship the Lord. Their worship grew out of the foundational knowledge that God was the basis of all life, the rock of everything. Their worship continued with the knowledge that God was the redeemer of all things; time and pressure were not the end of the story lines. God had the power to redeem the times and pressures of human life and encompass them into God's very own being.

The psalmist prays, "Let the words of my mouth and the meditation of my heart be acceptable to you, O Lord, my rock and my redeemer," and we realize these attributes of God are not in opposition to one another. This God redeems our lives by taking upon himself all our times and all our pressures; these elements are preserved and shaped into a new story, the story of our salvation, the story of our becoming the very people of God. In the Hebrew mind-set, there are two things that are important to know about the opening of this prayer. First, words contain power. Speech, even human speech, has the power to curse or to bless. Knowing their power demands thoughtfulness so that the spoken word shapes and does not destroy. Second, the heart is the center of the human body, not the brain. The seat of all reason, the center of one's very being, was located in the heart. To pray, "Let the words of my mouth and the meditation of my heart be acceptable to you," was literally to ask for God's presence in the power of the spoken word and in the locus of the human heart. The psalmist knew that time and pressure had the power to corrode, but God alone as rock and redeemer had the power to shape these elements into a story of triumph and salvation.

Our reading of the Old Testament provides invitation to take out our magnifying glasses and press our noses against the lines contained by this Rock, the one who is our rock and our redeemer. As we trace our fingers over the text and are drawn into ancient story lines, we read stories of redemption and salvation and forgiveness. There are stories there, encrusted as fossils, that make us question as we feel their pain and suffering. Although these stories are embedded into our lives as well, God redeems them. We are assured by their stories that God is able to contain all our times and pressures as well.

New Testament Lesson

After the final no there comes a yes,
And on that yes the future world depends.
                              —*Wallace Stevens,*
                    "The Well Dressed Man With a Beard"[1]

*T*he revolt began with a soft-spoken no. It caught everyone by surprise, especially me. It was my first Sunday as a field education intern
at a church in New Jersey. To introduce me to the congregation, the
pastors suggested I lead the children's sermon and then be introduced
to the congregation in the announcements following. The passage that
Sunday was the story of the ten lepers, only one of whom returned to
Christ to give thanks. Slightly nervous about the children's sermon, I
spent long hours with a teacher friend to come up with a fail-safe plan.
"It will be wonderful," she encouraged. Looking back on it, I have no
idea how we intended this fail-safe plan of ours to work, though it
seemed perfect at the time. "A skit!" we decided after considering
all the options—some way of visually showing the one leper who
returned in thanksgiving.

"Would any of you like to be Jesus in our skit this morning?" I asked.
The children looked around at each other to see who would volunteer,
when one young towhead in the middle said, "No." The congregation laughed, pretty heartily I'd say, while I, attempting to ignore his
response, called on another to be Jesus. "Would any of you like to be
one of the lepers?" This time, the young blonde and his buddy beside

him piped up with a slightly louder "No." The congregation laughed again, the pastors too, but this time a little less enthusiastically.

My heart was pounding. Wanting to make a good impression, concerned about the viability of this fabulous play, yet stumbling over my words, I quickly lost control of the revolution. "All right let's . . . ," I began, when three or four gathered around the two boys joined in, "Nooo!" "Why don't we . . . ," I hopefully continued, when a growing crowd shouted, "Noooo." Soon, laughter in the church had completely dimmed. Here I was in the midst of the revolution with no positive way of directing the youthful energy. With every word I said, a growing circle of young children chanted "Nooooo" while their parents, the pastors, the congregation and I watched in disbelief.

Finally, there was nothing left to say, except for the requisite "Let's close in a prayer." The response was a "NOOOOO!" that shook the stained-glass windows and rattled even the most experienced of pastors behind me. I cannot remember exactly what I prayed. A friend suggested I should have prayed, "Dear God, Yes! Amen." But my mind was too blurred by the revolution to come up with anything witty. I wanted to crawl under the communion table, only to retreat after the service was over, but now here came the introduction to the congregation.

"Your new intern," the pastor smiled, "will be with us for the rest of the year serving in education and worship." I know the congregation was scared to death wondering what would happen next. I was grateful for the words the pastor went on to say as he began his sermon: "You know, sometimes we come to church and hear the gospel message and every fiber in our body wants to shout out NO to the challenge of the gospel and the claim that it makes on our lives. We are here to find encouragement and strength from Scripture and one another to have the courage to say yes."

The Gospel of Mark enters the canon with an infinite YES. "The beginning of the good news of Jesus Christ, the son of God . . ." heralds the author. This yes is so big, so good, so new and resounding that previous literary genres could not contain it. The writer of Mark does a new thing, inventing a new literary form, this "Gospel" to tell of the ultimate YES of Jesus Christ. Here on this earth of ours, the very flesh and blood of God will walk and talk and teach and heal.

Spirits leap, dreams are realized, and everything is changed as Christ walks along whispering, "Yes." As he encounters the hurts and needs and doubts of others, ears are awakened and eyes are opened.

But then this good news, God's very yes to the world, tells those he healed to keep the secret by not telling the good news of what has happened to them. While the demons and lepers are the ones who hear this whisper the most audibly, Christ's own disciples, his closest friends and confidants, appear to be the ones most confused by this illimitable yes. Governed by fear and not by faith, they panic in a storm at sea and accuse their friend of letting them perish. "Why are you afraid?" Christ asks. "Have you any faith?" And we hear the disappointment in his voice. Tired of traveling, they express exasperation when asked to feed a hungry crowd and beg Christ to send the multitude away to take care of themselves. The disciples fall asleep at Gethsemane, after Christ's simple request to stay awake. Peter's denial proves true before the cock has crowed. As we get further and further into this story, we have to wonder what the writer of Mark was thinking when he named this magnum opus "Gospel," because there doesn't seem to be much of anything good and new here. "You call this good news?" we want to ask the writer, and that is even before we've reached the end of the story.

If we trust the resources of the earliest texts, then there does not appear to be any good news when we reach the end of the story. There at 16:8 we are left with three women, an empty tomb, no resurrection sighting and the chilling words "And they said nothing to anyone, for they were afraid." However, the man dressed in white sitting in the empty tomb offers the hopeful words "Do not be alarmed; you are looking for Jesus of Nazareth, who was crucified. He has been raised; he is not here . . . but he is going ahead of you to Galilee; there you will see him, just as he told you." Certainly there is the promise of meeting Christ on the road ahead, but will the women move from their frozen places? Will they break the paralyzing force of their fear to reveal their discovery to anyone?

James Joyce ended his book *Ulysses* with the word "yes." His was a love story about deciding "yes" to take the leap of faith. Why couldn't the good news of the Gospel love story end with an affirmative leap of faith, a "Yes!"—a little pep talk to be good disciples, a cheer that motivates to go and fight the battle ahead. Why couldn't this Gospel end with an example of someone's faith that might motivate us, inspire us, encourage us? But this isn't how this paradoxical Gospel ends. We are left with the disciples' stifling immobility and the fact that "they were afraid."

If there is one thing the New Testament addresses, it is the reality of human fear. But most of the time, the reality of fear is partnered with a word of encouragement: "Do not fear." "Don't be afraid." Someone told me that 366 times in Scripture (one for every day of the year plus one for leap year) the expression "Do not be afraid" occurs. But there are no such words here in the Gospel of Mark. There is no affirmation of faith after the expression of disbelief, no assurance of pardon following the confession, no blessing following the charge.

If Mark's Gospel leaves us to grapple with the abstract reality of fear made real in our lives, then the Gospel of John leaves us to grapple with the physical manifestations of that fear. The verse in John that we all memorized in Sunday school and that now appears everywhere, from posters displayed at ball games to "In and Out Burger" cups to bumper stickers, is the familiar John 3:16 that sums up the mystery of the gospel: "For God so loved the world that he gave his only begotten Son, so that everyone who believes in him may not perish but have eternal life." While these words resonate with the mystery and glory of the incarnation, perhaps even more mysterious are the words just preceding them: "And just as Moses lifted up the serpent in the wilderness, so must the Son of Man be lifted up," leaving the reader to grapple with this snake, wondering how these two disparate stories are related. The common denominator is fear. Everyone bitten by those fearful snakes in the wilderness were made to look straight in the face of what they were most afraid of as they gazed upon a serpent of bronze posted on a pole. As someone who goes to sleep each night wondering if there are scorpions in my bed sheets, I am grateful not to have a bronzed scorpion raised high in my bedroom. I don't want to gaze upon my fears so graphically. Yet the writer of John connects this to the resurrection. By his doing this we realize he knows our very human fears of the power of a God who can manifest a bodily resurrection. From this point on in the Gospel of John, the writer tells of character after character who must look his and her deepest fears in the face. This God is not one to be messed with or run away from, and yet our human fear response is to dart away as quickly as possible.

There is a proverb that claims, "Fear discovers a hundred ways of escape." Human response to fear in the Gospels adds dozens to the hundred: asking questions not to create understanding but to put up defenses, drawing boundaries, laying claim, denying in betrayal, speculating about the future, conspiring, deserting, mocking, taunting, fleeing, remaining quiet. Our fear of a God who knows the fleshy walk and talk of human nature, our fear of a God who can overcome betrayal and death, our fear of a God who is infinite and full of YES is overwhelming. We find a hundred ways of escape, even though this is the God whom we desire and need the very most. Anything new and deep and transforming raises fear and prompts the question, Will grace meet us on the road ahead? We are fearful of persecution, fearful of transformation, and, most of all, fearful of resurrection. Our fears prevent us from full trust and belief and surrender.

A wise pastor once said, "Fear is false evidence that appears real." Like a good pastor, he repeated it again so our ears would be awakened: "FEAR is False Evidence that Appears Real." His clever acronym has rung true for me every day since. But in the New Testament, fear does not come from false evidence that appears real. Fear comes from *real* evidence that proves everything else false. "Do not be alarmed; you are looking for Jesus of Nazareth, who was crucified. He has been raised; he is not here . . . but he is going ahead of you to Galilee; there you will see him, just as he told you." In the Gospel of Mark, there might not be a resurrection appearance, but even more so there is the promise of Christ's appearance. Christ will meet you on the road ahead.

The writer of Mark had a clear intention of just how this story should end. The response to this real evidence is left up to us. Will we add to the list of one hundred ways to escape? Will we close the book and pretend it made no difference in our lives? Will we join those voices that cry out, "No"?

Though there is silence at the end of the story, we know the real evidence says, "Christ is not here. He is risen. He will meet you on the road ahead." Just as this New Testament book comes to a close, I hear an echo. I hear after the silence the soft whisper of an echo that sounds something like a voice spoken over a stormy sea. "Why are you afraid? Have you any faith?" I know then that Mark knew exactly how the story would end. As Wallace Stevens would say, "After the final no there comes a yes, / And on that yes the future world depends."

We call that good news? Yes. It is from here that God's revolution begins so that we might live out a new testament. The whole future depends on our living out that new testament—a testament that overcomes silence and resounds with an overpowering YES.

Sermon

One good word is bread for a thousand.
                                   —*David Whyte, "Loaves and Fishes"*[1]

*T*housands of crumbs were scattered across the park. Or should I say, they were scattered down the hill, across the lawn, around a tree, around another tree, down the pier toward the lake and back up again, along the shoreline then back toward the trees. So entranced was I by the crumbs, it took me a few minutes to notice the young girl whose hand had carefully laid them out. I watched as she continued to spread out this feast for the ducks, and then smiled as I heard her shout out one good word: "Dinnertime!" Such a sweet word may never again be said so prayerfully and joyfully to a gaggle of ducks.

To move from ducks and bread crumbs to a congregation and sermon is a difficult homiletical move. Preaching professors would quickly advise caution. The picture could easily lead us astray. Just who are the ducks? What are the crumbs? And how are we called to follow their convoluted yet nourishing path? Yet something about that scene I witnessed comes to mind when I reflect on preaching the Word of God. For both the preacher and the hearer, how does word become bread? What do preachers provide? What do worshipers hold onto? How does one good word about the Word himself become bread for a thousand in the sermon? How in that preaching moment does the interaction of preacher and listener become the bread of life?

Anyone who has ever baked bread knows that simply combining the ingredients doesn't always make for a fine loaf of bread. In fact, most of my bread-making experiences have led to loaves as hard as hockey pucks. The problem with my bread making is in my kneading and my patience in its rising. After the hockey-puck disaster, experienced bread makers from my church invited me over to their home at Christmas for a lesson. There at the island of their kitchen, the only kitchen where I have ever stood next to a hearth, I learned the secrets of bread making from hands that have lovingly performed this art many times. I had been combining the ingredients correctly, but my hands had not yet learned the secret to kneading; we have lost the art of getting our hands dusty in flour, ready to use the rhythms of our bodies to knead the dough. And my heart had not yet mastered the patience of allowing the dough time to rise. In a world of bread-making machines, Wonder Bread and lots of impatience, kneading and rising are lost skills. Kneading and rising were the elements missing from my bread making, and they are often the elements missing in the preaching moment.

As someone who has been on both sides of the pulpit, I see these missing elements in both places. As a listener, there are times when I have thrown my fists at a sermon without giving it the gentle kneading that it deserved. There are Sundays when I desperately want to walk away from worship having gotten something "out" of a sermon instead of being patient to the Spirit's rising in my heart as the sermon is lived out in the intermixing of the Word with my week. In his book *How to Worship as a Presbyterian*, Dean Chapman offers ways the listener can be active in the preaching process. Instead of coming to worship expecting a sermon just to happen, he challenges us to engage in a prayerful process of preparing for the sermon. His steps for bread making include reading the Scripture before Sunday morning; praying for the preacher's engagement with the text; opening up the Bible on Sunday morning to follow along with the Scripture proclaimed; listening to the sermon, perhaps even taking notes; discussing the sermon not in a reactive way but in a prayerful way in small groups.[2] Listening calls for kneading the text in a slow and gentle way that takes longer than a few minutes for the first time on a Sunday morning. Listening well demands that some of the critiques and distractions recede, giving way to the Spirit's rising.

As a preacher, I know the ways a preacher can resist the transformative process. I don't always have time to give the process the attention it deserves. I take shortcuts exegetically to prove the point I want to make. I avoid engaging the text in a personal way because sometimes it is too painful to go there. I pound out a sermon at the computer in an hour in between hospital visits and meetings, instead of giving it the time it needs to rise.

How does a pastor find time amid the demands of ministry for kneading and rising? How does she find the right word? How, in a noisy fast-paced world with people who want answers, does he balance between speech and silence? How can a sermon be both contemporary in style and yet grounded in tradition? How does a sermon address the needs of a congregation and yet not shy away from the demanding biblical texts that many feel they don't need to hear? How does a sermon rise above the many competing voices in the minds of those who are listening—the voices that critique, the voices that compile to-do lists, the voices that think they don't need to listen? These are just a few of the homiletical issues that get stirred into the mix every Sunday morning, and yet somehow each week the preacher, knowing all this, sits down with text in hand, to listen prayerfully for the one good word God would have her provide for the congregation.

With such issues at hand, it would be easy to rely on the mechanics a simple sermon outline might provide, or to put trust in the Internet story that arrives in your mailbox like a deus ex machina in a Greek tragedy. But relying on quick fixes turns the sermon into a prepackaged cake mix rather than warm, nourishing bread that has undergone the transformative process. A search committee from a local congregation divided into teams to go out to different churches for worship on a Sunday morning. When they met together, they discovered that many of them had heard similar sermons. While it's one thing to hear the similarity of a lectionary-based biblical text, it is quite another to hear from the lectionary of stories that had been provided by an Internet preaching service. How is one to believe then that the pastor had opened himself to the process of kneading the text and giving rise to the Spirit?

Too many Sundays I hear sermons where I experience the preached word as disembodied. The preacher seems to have no emotive reaction to the issues raised or the questions asked. While there is a fine line between letting the sermon be more about you than the text, we do believe that God speaks to us through an incarnate word. If that word is incarnate, that means it has been engaged in the life and thought of the preacher. Some Sundays I leave wanting to ask, How did this text touch your life this week as you prayerfully lived with it? How did it intersect with the roads you travel in your day-to-day life?

Then there are the sermons that provide all of the answers, carefully pressed and laid out, leaving me no room to ponder the questions first and then imagine the answers. Other sermons desperately try to fill up each second within the given time frame with words chosen more to fill the gap than to lead the worshiper into the meaning within the text. As Barbara Brown Taylor writes, "Sometimes I think we do all the talking because we are afraid God won't. Or, conversely, that God will. Either way, staying preoccupied with our own words seems a safer bet than opening ourselves up either to God's silence or God's speech, both of which have the power to undo us."[3] When we rely on any of these mechanisms to preach, we produce those dreaded hockey pucks that, when tossed out into the congregation, have the force to deaden and numb rather than nourish and feed.

Christ knew how to take one good word and turn it into bread for a thousand. Five loaves and two fish were all the illustrations he required. His sermons were as restrained as "I am the bread of life," and as silent as a line drawn in the sand. Christ's preaching allowed the hearer to enter in imaginatively to a process where given just a little yeast and a little flour a new and needed vision of the kingdom of God might rise to the hearer's understanding. Christ kneaded the words of God by exploring the meaning of the ancient texts in his given context. The Spirit gave rise to new ways of hearing God's words through the Word in active engagement with people in need.

The ingredients for sermon making are all there—text, context, subtext. Who needs flour and sugar when substances as rich as these are available? The biblical text in its infinite variety and ultimate truth, as well as the unique contexts of our congregations and even the personal faith journey of the pastor, provide plenty for preachers to work their hands into. Even those underlying subtexts—the doubts and questions and disagreements that any active listener may have in listening to a sermon—can be effectively met and overcome through a sermon that honors the listener's engagement. When these things are mixed and kneaded together, hand over hand, with the force of a body that is prayerfully involved in its making, bread for the multitudes is easily made.

In a series of lectures at Princeton Seminary, Fred Craddock said that the task of a good sermon is to "make the absent present." To me that sounds like bread making at its best. You can mix up some flour and yeast, sugar and baking powder, but this mix becomes bread only through a mysterious transformative process invisible to the eye. It is a process that makes the absent present. An absent biblical world becomes present to a modern-day struggle. An absent fruit of the Spirit becomes present through the Word proclaimed. An absent word of justice is made present to an oppressive situation. Craddock's words give the preacher a starting place when prayerfully reading the biblical text to ask, What is absent in the faith lives of this congregation that could be made present through the preaching of this text?

Another theologian who provides insight into bread making is James E. Loder. In *The Transforming Moment*, he examines how the seemingly absent Holy Spirit is made present through the ongoing movement of the spirit within the human soul. In this work he describes a process of transformation not intended for sermon making or bread baking, but one that still manages to speak to both. He describes five steps: a conscious conflict in the human soul in wrestling with the Word of God, a period of scanning as one looks for answers, a moment of "A-ha" in the search that brings insight to the conflict, a period of release and repatterning as the insight evokes change, and a final period of interpretation as the repatterning takes deeper root in daily life.[4] This process is one that honors the need and gives room for the kneading. The steps described allow for the rise of understanding through patient listening and searching that ultimately emerge in a new life transformed. A sermon, preached with integrity and heard with an open heart, has the potential to make for real change in a worshiping life. And that is a life that can nourish thousands.

What I want to say to preachers is twofold: be restrained in the kneading and be open to the rising that the meaning of the text might have for you. Be open to this process of transformation that when undertaken will provide nourishment not just for your congregation, but also for you and for this world. Be open to what may be absent in your own faith journey becoming present through your prayerfully living with the Word of God.

During World War II, many children were orphaned by the devastation of war and persecution. They were on a journey they didn't choose, relying on crumbs. Communities across Europe took these children in—offering them a safe haven, for at least a time. When the children arrived, they were scared to death. Even though they were assigned to homes, had warm beds and full meals, anxieties about their past invaded their sleep. Fears of being uprooted, fears of no food, fears of yet another loss were all pervading. Unable to sleep, they became more and more worked up. Finally—I don't know who thought of it or how—someone came up with a saving revelation. The adopted families began giving the orphaned children pieces of bread to hold onto while they slept at night. It worked. What was given to them was just a crumb, but it got them through the long dark nights. The children slept with those crumbs given to them and held onto them for dear life.

After using this illustration in a sermon on a recent Sunday morning, another pastor from our church and an elder went the next day to offer Communion to a woman dying of cancer. She had been a member of the church for over thirty life-giving years, and we all were grieved by the speed at which her cancer spread. While a week earlier she had been up and around, talkative and with color in her cheeks, now she was unable to partake of the bread and the wine offered in Communion. At first the elder asked the pastor, "What should we do?" Then in a moment, her question answered itself as she said, "We should tuck it into her hand." So the two of them dropped a bit of wine onto her lips and gently tucked the crumbs into her hands. There a sermon was offered, one good piece of the Word that might just turn into bread for a thousand as Carol passed from this life into the next.

As a church we need to think about what bread we are tucking into the hands of those who need God's Word the most. A word of tenderness, a morsel of kindness, a crumb of mercy, a taste of justice. These are the words that nourish and feed; they are also the words that multiply and feed the hungry.

Responding

Responding

*I am seeking perhaps what Socrates asked for
in the prayer from the* Phaedrus *when he said,
"May the outward and inward man be at one."
I would like to achieve a state of inner spiritual
grace from which I could function and give as
I was meant to in the eye of God.*
> —Anne Morrow Lindbergh, Gift from the Sea[1]

*H*aving heard the gospel proclaimed through Scripture, sermon and song, the next movement of worship invites us to respond. Our response in worship comes in the form of our prayers, our offering, our affirmations of faith and our songs. Though these responses are part of our worship, we know we are truly leading a worshiping life when they become as natural as our very walking. Unfortunately for me such a transition doesn't always come so naturally. Instead, I turn away from the inward me toward outward possibilities of avoidance and desire. I don't always like who I am inside, which makes it hard to achieve a state of inner spiritual grace, let alone try and "function and give as I was meant to in the eye of God." Either my inside hopes and desires don't match up with my outward living, or my outward attempts to respond to grace don't correspond to my inward guilt and anxiety. I spend my days in conflict, walking away from self, walking away from others, walking away from grace.

Yet we are called to respond. To function, as Anne Morrow Lindbergh says, as we were meant to in the eye of God. To give. To muster up something to offer the world and to live up to the challenge of the gospel. The question of response is ultimately a question of vocation. How are we called to live our lives so that we do please God? Frederick Buechner tries to answer this question in a way that aims to bring the outward and the inner person together. He is often quoted as saying, "The place God calls you to is the place where your deep gladness and the world's deep hunger meet."[2] In other words, you will be in turmoil in your inner being if the place where you try and serve does not bring you a sense of joy. In turn, the world will be in turmoil if we don't try and put our gifts into action in a way that meets the needs of the world.

As much as I like Buechner's words, something is missing from them for me. Certainly I want my response to bubble up from a place of joy within, but if that is the only criteria for vocation, then there are parts of me that are left out of my response. Those are the parts where I have experienced pain and hurt, regret and longing. Those are the places where the gospel has had to ebb away at the painful parts of life and slowly toss and turn in the surf of my soul until something a little more polished and smooth emerges.

If Paul had responded only from a place of joy, we might not have found him sitting in prison or shipwrecked or striding on even as he felt a pain in his side. He could have written letters from home and saved himself from a whole lot of suffering. Sure the gospel would have been preached, but absent from that word would have been the walk of his life.

In Philippians 4:9 Paul provides some insight to the prospects of our response to the gospel. The preceding words to this verse are the more noted "Rejoice in the Lord always: again I will say, Rejoice." Certainly he is calling for our response to come forth out of joy. He continues, "Do not worry about anything . . . whatever is true, whatever is honorable, whatever is just, whatever is pure, whatever is pleasing, whatever is commendable, if there is any excellence and if there is anything worthy of praise, think about these things." Here too Paul wants our outward actions to match our inward thoughts. Then he says these words: "Whatever you have seen and heard and experienced and learned in me, put them into practice."[3]

Paul is prompting our response. It is a response that grows out of learning from his life and his encounter with the gospel of Jesus Christ. It is a call for us to go through the same manner of reflection in regard to our lives—what have I seen and heard? What have I experienced and learned? How can I put these things into practice in a way that brings me joy and meets the needs of the world? It is an incredible call, an invitation to reflect on what we have seen and heard and experienced and learned in our lives and then to put these revelations into a gospel response.

Paul is someone who knows firsthand about the ups and downs in the walk of life. Paul could easily say, I am someone who has *seen* people die because of my persecution of them, I have *heard* people think I was crazy for having this blinding light experience, I have *experienced* difficult times while in prison, but in the midst of this all I have *learned* of the incredible goodness of God and the mercy of Jesus Christ.

This verse is about our vocation. It is about what we do with our lives—as parents, as pastors, as employees, as retirees, as students. How can you take what you have seen and heard, experienced and learned—all of the good and the bad, all of the joys and the regrets— and put these things into practice into a response that will be pleasing in the eyes of God?

So often we don't want to put into practice the experiences of our lives. We would rather run from them, forget them, bury or push them aside. I can imagine Paul felt this way at times—embarrassed, guilty and shameful. He could have easily run from his past, ignored it, denied it and buried it. But instead he transforms what he has seen and heard, experienced and learned in his lifetime into a response that achieves for him a state of inner spiritual grace from which he can function and give as he was meant to in the eye of God.

The blockbuster novel *The Divine Secrets of the Ya-Ya Sisterhood* led to the formation of Ya-Ya groups all over the country. Women came together in small groups out of a deep connection to the book. One of the places where I connected in reading the story was in the character of Sidda, who struggled with the tough experiences of her life. Sidda worked in the theater and had a difficult relationship with her alcoholic mother. Time and time again, her mother embarrassed Sidda with her drinking. Time and time again, Sidda tried to hide the obvious signs of her mother's drinking problem.

One of the final blows comes at a party after a huge opening of Sidda's most recent play. Her mother creates quite a scene in the midst of many prominent people, mortifying Sidda on this critical opening night. In a last attempt to hide her mother's drinking problem, Sidda's good friend Wade escorts her mother out of the room so Sidda can entertain her guests. After the party Sidda goes to Wade's home to check on her mother and finds her passed out on the sofa. Relieved, Sidda thanks Wade. Instead of saying the expected "You're welcome," Wade surprised Sidda with these words: "Use it."

"Use it," he said. "Use everything in your life to create your art."[4] This divine secret is the same message of Paul at Philippi. Do not be ashamed of your past; do not try and push your past aside; don't ignore the experiences of your life—use them. Put them into practice. Give them as an offering. What do I do with my life? Use the experiences—the good and the bad. Put these into practice in response to the gospel.

Recently I saw an incredible exhibit of nature photos taken around the United States. Reading about the photographer, I learned that he was a truck driver. Intrigued by his story, I invited him out for coffee. James looks less like a trucker and much more like Bill Gates. But then again, everything about his story was surprising. He described going through a tough time a few years ago, things he would "rather not talk about," he explained. Wanting some time alone and some time to reflect, he went through the process to become a truck driver. Out on the open road, not only did he find the needed respite he had hoped for, but he also discovered incredible beauty. "I had the opportunity to see the best of our country. I would get the first glimpse of wildflowers, fall foliage, the sun setting over mountains. The beauty was incredible and I wanted to share it with others who weren't as fortunate." Having taken a class in photography when he was in high school, he dug out his camera from his closet and started taking photographs. Within months, the back of the cab of his eighteen-wheeler had turned into a photography lab.

Wanting to share what he had seen, he put together a catalog of photos and gave them to Deacon Ministries and Stephen's Ministries in local churches. There he trained volunteers to take the catalogs to the homebound and the hospitalized and invite them to choose a photograph that gives them a glimpse of hope. Once their pictures are selected, he sends them blown up and framed, ready to be hung so that God's beauty might be seen. His ministry certainly begins at the intersection of joy and need, but even more so it grows out of what he has seen and heard, experienced and learned in his life. Life can be hard and lonely, glimpses of God can be difficult to see, beauty is rare and fleeting—all the more reason to make sure his photographs get into the hands of those who need them the most. "Use it," Wade says, and James certainly does.

The invitation to put our life into practice does not just come at the individual level. As a corporate body, we are called to reflect on what we have seen and heard, experienced and learned together as the body of Christ and then respond to that reflection in a way that pleases God. A church I served in New Jersey knew of the struggle the daughter of their senior pastor had faced with alcohol and drug abuse. Like the ebb and flow of the tide at the Jersey shore, hope and disappointment came and went in ongoing cycles. There were periods of sobriety and long months of disappearance. The congregation journeyed with the pastor and his family through the awful struggle and eventual death as a result of his daughter's addiction. The congregation saw the ups and downs, heard the despair, experienced the letdowns and learned much about the demons of addiction. Then, as a corporate body, they put all of this into practice. An incredible ministry of twelve-step programs filled the halls of the church. Overeaters Anonymous, Sexaholics Anonymous and Alcoholics Anonymous all had a place there. Men and women from the congregation who had never owned up to their struggles found the courage to do so. Gamblers who had lost fortunes and spouses discovered a place to begin again.

Paul calls us to wrestle as individuals and as a church with our response to the gospel and with our response to the things we have seen and heard, experienced and learned in our lives. We are challenged to look at the walk of our lives just as he used the journey of his life to call others to respond to the gospel. In a similar vein, the psalmist calls us to do the same. There may be no greater words in the Bible than those of Psalm 23. They have provided comfort to generations. The words of the psalmist are a testimony to what the psalmist himself had seen and heard, experienced and learned in the walk of his life.

> The Lord is my shepherd, I shall not want.
> He makes me lie down in green pastures;
> He leads me beside still waters;
> He restores my soul.
> He leads me in right paths for his name's sake.
>
> Even though I walk through the darkest valley,
> I fear no evil; for you are with me;
> Your rod and your staff—they comfort me.
>
> You prepare a table for me in the presence of my enemies;
> You anoint my head with oil; my cup overflows.
> Surely goodness and mercy shall follow me all the days of
>   my life,
> And I shall dwell in the house of the Lord my whole life long.

The psalmist describes a long walk through pastures, along the water, through dark valleys, and we know from his words that the experiences of his life were not always easy. He grieved, he tripped, he lost and he suffered. But we also know this—on that long walk he *saw* a table prepared for him, he *heard* a voice say "do not fear," he *experienced* a constant companion and he *learned* that the goodness and mercy of the Lord would follow him all the days of his life. He takes what he has seen and heard, experienced and learned in the long journey—the long walk of his life—and he uses them. He puts them into practice.

There is an old story from South Africa about a teacher who sent his student to the shore. The teacher told the student that he had a gift for her there. In order to get the gift, she was given a set of instructions as to where to walk to receive it. The student walked along still waters, rocky paths, and deep valleys and across plain fields. She met kind people on the journey and she had some troubling encounters. Along the way she experienced calamities, adventures and loneliness. After a very long walk, she came to the shore of the ocean.

There on the beach, exactly where the teacher had described, was a gift—a beautiful shell. The student picked it up, tucked it into her pocket and began the long walk home. She experienced adventure, grace, kindness and rudeness along the journey home. She said to her teacher upon returning, "Thank you for the wonderful gift of the shell, but why the long walk there?" The teacher responded, "The long walk was part of the gift as well."

Each one of us has a unique walk, a walk filled with calamity and adventure, grace and misfortune, the kindness of strangers and the betrayal of friends. We have all seen and heard and experienced and learned unique things in the course of our lifetimes. Each of us has had a unique encounter with the gospel of Jesus Christ.

In *Gift from the Sea*, Anne Morrow Lindbergh reflects on the ebb and flow of her life as she spends a summer at the shore. Having lost a husband and a son, she goes to heal at the seashore and is surprised to find herself writing down her reflections. Picking up seashell after seashell, she shares what she has learned in her life. She had no idea then, as she wrote for herself, how her grief and her hope would ultimately speak to many. In her writing, the prayer she offers from *Phaedrus* finds an answer, that as she reconciled her inward self and her outward self, she would be able to "function and give as I was meant to in the eye of God."

What I have learned as I have struggled with how to reconcile my inward self and outward self is that I have to dredge up all of the stuff of my life, hold it in my hand and look at it anew. There I see an incredible shell—it is made up of what I have *S*een, *H*eard, *E*xperienced and *L*earned in my *L*ife. Its creation has taken years and has become more beautiful in the pummeling of the tide. This is my SHELL to give in response to the gospel. I offer it in prayer, in affirmation, in offering and in mission. The long walk of our lives is very much a part of the gift as well, when we have the eyes to see it as God does. It truly is a gift from the sea.

Affirmation of Faith

"Here I am," said I to the chaos.

—Life Is Beautiful

*T*hese opening words to the movie *Life Is Beautiful* are so subtle I missed them on the first viewing. Guido, played by Roberto Benigni, and his friend are driving along on a carefree day in their convertible jalopy as the friend recites a poem. With English subtitles at the bottom of the screen and opening credits displayed in the middle, I almost missed these important words: "I sing what I see, nothing gets by me. 'Here I am,' said I to the chaos." The words certainly describe the decision Guido makes in the movie in how to respond to the chaos around him. Faced with a world gone mad, Guido learns firsthand the horrors of the Holocaust.

The movie is impossible to describe. A lighthearted look at life in a concentration camp? The love of a father for his son? A romantic tale of passion and loss? No words come close to describing the movie, except these: "Here I am, said I to the chaos."

Every Sunday in worship in response to the gospel being proclaimed, we affirm what we believe. Some Sundays that affirmation is my saying to the chaos of the world, "Here I am and it is upon these things that I stand." Then there are other Sundays when it's not quite so clear to me. In the midst of the murk it is God who speaks to me with a faithful and resolute "Here I am, Lisa, for you and your children, for the world in which you live, even in the midst of its chaos."

In working with churches in small groups for a workshop on worship, I have heard varying responses to the saying of the Affirmation of Faith. A few are often unwilling to even utter the words: "I'm not sure I fully believe them. How can I say these words with honesty?" Others have the opposite response: "I say the Affirmation of Faith with hope and a prayer that I might live into their meaning." Both are faithful responses. The ones I worry about are those who say these prayers routinely and without thought.

In an effort to unpack the Affirmation of Faith, with the hope of making it less routine, one theology professor calls upon her Theology 101 class to look at the Apostles' Creed line by line. "Put a check next to the lines you can say you fully believe," she instructs. "Put an X next to the lines you do not believe. Then put a question mark next to the ones you have a question about." With her assignment, the creed that had been heralded as unquestionable suddenly becomes real and relevant. Why is it so wonderfully refreshing to have a conversation with the creeds rather than utter them routinely?

Studying the creed line by line, students realize each claim is a claim against chaos. "I believe in God the Father Almighty." God's might topples chaos. "Maker of heaven and earth" is an affirmation of God's creation from the primordial chaos. Even the assertion "I believe in the holy catholic church" is a claim against the chaos that divides us into denominations and instead affirms that we are one universal church, no chaos here.

Even in a post–9-11 world when we struggle to convince our kids and our congregations that the world is not falling to pieces, we really don't know chaos. Even though my life seems in disarray at times, there is no comparison to the evil others have faced. John McCain is someone who knows from experience. Held prisoner of war in Vietnam for more years than he cares to remember, he daily had to seek an affirmation of faith to help him survive his turmoil. He found that affirmation made visible when he was thrown into solitary confinement in a 6-by-9-foot hole in the ground. He said, "On the wall was etched a testimony, scratched into stone by a previous occupant: 'I believe in God, the Father Almighty,' read the jagged writing."[1] The words said to a lonely God-forsaken soul, "Here I am."

A young friend of mine was desperately listening to hear God say the words "Here I am." He was a self-proclaimed atheist. His atheism and antireligious views stemmed from anger in his personal life. He had been born with a heart defect. Friendships and schooling were always interrupted by heart surgeries. His weak heart hampered the possibility of team sports and athletic pursuits. He felt discouraged and angry much of the time. He spoke about some of this during his year in confirmation class. Others in the class heard his pain and suffering and met him there. We were all surprised at the end of the year not only when he had decided to join the church, but also when he read to the class his affirmation of faith. He described how he had discovered a sense of thanksgiving over the course of the year. It wasn't the kind of thanksgiving he had expected—thanksgiving for being healed or for being able to play basketball—but a thanksgiving for daily life. A joy in the ordinary. A sense that life was beautiful. He went on to quote these words he discovered on an Internet search: "An atheist's worst day is when he wants to say thank you and realizes he has no one to say thank you to." It was this recognition, the young man said, that helped him to acknowledge God's presence. "Here I am," God whispers in surprising ways. So in turn we can say thank you.

In her latest book of essays, *Small Wonder*, Barbara Kingsolver describes her process of grief after September 11: "Sometimes writing seemed to be all that kept me from falling apart in the face of so much death and anguish, the one alternative to weeping without cease."[2] Her writing led her to "cataloging" a list of sorts, of small wonders she found as alternatives to the violence and the grief. These wonders became small affirmations of faith. She goes on to conclude,

> Small change, small wonders—these are the currency of my endurance and ultimately of my life. . . . I have stories of things I believe in: a persistent river, a forest on the edge of night, the religion inside of a seed, the startle of wingbeats when a spark of red life flies against all reason out of darkness. One child, one bear. I'd like to speak of small wonders, and the possibility of taking heart.[3]

These stories are all affirmations of faith: jagged words etched in stone, a quote found on the Internet, small wonders, and yet still we come to the words of affirmation in worship on a Sunday morning and it can sound so routine. We don't really have words for the affirmations of faith, those huge leaps across the chaos we make in our own lives. We need help seeing and saying so these words are not just theological jargon, but words that connect and have meaning.

A colleague uses the following technique to make the connection. With the Brief Statement of Faith of the Presbyterian Church (U.S.A.) in one hand and a stack of movies in the other, she asks adults and youth alike to look for the affirmations of faith present in the movie clips. Playing anything from *The Wedding Singer* to *Shawshank Redemption*, *Legally Blonde* and *Remember the Titans*, she has the group read one of the sections of the Brief Statement of Faith first. The Sunday I was there, we read the portion on the Holy Spirit that goes like this:

We trust in God the Holy Spirit,
Everywhere the giver and renewer of life.
The Spirit justifies us by grace through faith,
Sets us free to accept ourselves and to love God and
neighbor,
And binds us together with all believers
In the one body of Christ, the Church.
The same Spirit
Who inspired the prophets and apostles
Rules our faith and life in Christ through Scripture,
Engages us through the Word proclaimed,
Claims us in the waters of baptism,
Feeds us with the bread of life and the cup of salvation,
And calls women and men to all ministries of the Church.
In a broken and fearful world
The Spirit gives us courage
To pray without ceasing,
To witness among all peoples to Christ as Lord and Savior,
To unmask idolatries in church and culture,
To hear the voices of peoples long silenced,
And to work with others for justice, freedom and peace.
In gratitude to God, empowered by the Spirit,
We strive to serve Christ in our daily tasks
And to live holy and joyful lives,
Even as we watch for God's new heaven and new earth,
Praying, "Come, Lord Jesus!"[4]

Then with pen in hand and movie on screen, the group gathered is asked to watch in the visual parable for examples of an affirmation made in the statement. Suddenly, the words have meaning. Then names of other movies and scenes are offered as connections to the creed. Out of the chaos of words and images, the Holy Spirit is revealed in new and surprising ways, crying out, "Here I am; how come you didn't see me before?"

Learning the creeds of the church is important. Seeing their connections to our lives and world is vital. But we also need to be challenged to write our own personal affirmations of faith. Session members yearly challenge confirmation students to the difficult task of writing their statement of faith. Pick up a pen and put this stuff into your own words is the command, but there is never a turning of the tables when our youth ask the elders to hear their own. Mr. Charles, let's hear about what you have come to believe in the course of your lifetime. Mrs. Clifton, tell me how you have faith amid the chaos of life. We Presbyterians shy away from these sorts of testimonials, and at what great loss.

When he was announced as the winner of an Academy Award for *Life Is Beautiful*, Roberto Benigni bounded across the backs of the seats, creating an unforgettable Oscar moment. No one will ever forget the joy with which he leapt chair over chair to the stage. In the movie, the leap of faith is not in his step, but in his eyes. While his actions and words displayed steely resolve to protect his young son, the viewer sees the leap of faith present in his eyes. We know that leap as we affirm in the midst of evil that life, indeed, is beautiful. We know that leap when we look desperately, gropingly, for small wonders. We know that leap, unbounded by doubt, unfettered by chaos, that comes to us quietly, faithfully, hopefully and affirms, "Here I am."

Middle Hymn

You can sing in those low times,
in abandoned, love-spent sorrow,
or in praise for something so simple
and wondrous as the sun rising.
But it's just not the same—
not the same as a song sung for you,
a soft drift off to sleep melody offered
as a gift, an amulet, a blessing
floating down.
Oh, I love to be carried that way
even off-key, the words misplaced, forgotten,
but so perfect in its giving,
the songs of comfort in the dark,
in fever, or in fear,
songs as offering, as armor, as hands raised,
doors flung open, as a place to rest, to triumph,
to dream.

—*Jennifer Roberts, "You Can Sing"*[1]

*W*hen I need a song of comfort in the dark, I turn to the Psalms. Turning toward the middle of the Bible, sometimes my finger rests upon a psalm of praise; other days it's a psalm of lament. No matter where my spirit rests, either psalm helps me to drift off to sleep. The peace comes from knowing that each is a song sung for me—each is a gift, an amulet, a blessing. There are days when I need to be carried that way, and many others when I read the psalm as a prayer for someone

89

I know who needs comfort. Just as the psalm sings for me, I sing on for those who can't sing for themselves this day.

Recently a family friend died of cancer. She was too young to die. She left two teenaged children, a vibrant career and a strong marriage. She was faithful to her church and dedicated to her community; it was a tremendous loss for everyone. My sister-in-law was enraged at God. "If that were me being taken up prematurely to heaven and made to leave all those who make love real," she ranted. "I would have a little talk with God. I'd walk into those pearly gates and tell God, 'There is no way, Lord, I'm singing in that angel choir. I just don't have any hallelujahs in me right now.'" Her rant rang true for all who knew the tragedy. Sometimes we just don't have any hallelujahs in us. Whether in heaven or on earth, our souls just can't muster up that bit of praise and prayer in song. It's not that we don't care for music; it's that we don't care for the circumstances and situations of our lives and world. There are the dark chords of despair and hunger, poverty and loneliness, angst and anger that sound so loud within our souls we can't hear the notes of anything else. You want me to sing? I just don't have it in me, Lord. There is discord in my life and in our world. No hallelujahs here; someone else can sing them for now.

While life can be discordant, we still are not comfortable with the minor key. We want to avoid the dissonance by lingering in the harmony of the major keys. Some churches have passed resolutions not to sing songs in a minor key. Too many complaints were heard by the pastors and the music committees about the choice of songs. But for those who want to acknowledge the dissonance, offering only praise-filled songs in a major key doesn't give permission to lament. Where in worship is it acceptable for grief and anguish to be voiced? For those who show up on Sunday morning expecting to open themselves to worship as they sing the opening hymn, there are some days when singing "Hallelujah" can feel jarring.

Visiting a small rural church while on a mission trip in West Virginia, I praised the beauty of a "Hallelujah!" banner sewn by members of the congregation. The letters leapt and curled off the felt, conveying a joy and energy only the best artisans could achieve. While finely done, the banner bore the wear and tear of many years. The pastor went on to explain to me a wonderful service centered around the banner. On the last Sunday before Lent, the congregation participates in a "Burial of the Hallelujah" service. The liturgy shouts, "Take the Hallelujah from us." It continues, "Take down the colors of rejoicing and replace them with purple—the color of penitence and preparation." Then the banner is removed from the sanctuary until the trumpet swells of Easter morning beckon the procession, led by the banner, back into the sanctuary. Throughout the Lenten season many churches do not mention the word "hallelujah." Not in the Gloria, not in the doxology, not in prayer or Scripture or hymn.

Sarah, a friend and pastor, lost her son ten days after his birth. She needed permission to bury her hallelujahs. He died suddenly, after a routine checkup with the doctor, due to a complication with his heart. All were shocked. She realized how many times as a pastor she had said to someone, "You are going to get through this," or "Your grief will last for a season and then you will know hope." After facing serious loss for herself for the first time, she wanted to go back and retrieve all those words. She realized she had not been comfortable dwelling with others in their pain and suffering. She uttered words from that place of discomfort. Having gone through the depths herself she wanted to go back to them and say less and simply be with them more. She realized what she needed wasn't hope; the hope was there, though buried deep. What she needed, and what she now would offer in her ministry, was permission to be in that dark place. She needed assurance that the despair was an acceptable place to dwell for the time being.

A few years ago in a senior high Sunday school class we were discussing the kingdom of God. Set out before the class were fifty or so images of places, people and things. The class was asked to pick out an image that described what the kingdom of God was like for them. The class chose scenes of edenic tranquility and of parental comraderie. But it was Adrian's choice that struck me deeply. He picked an image of a perfect snowy winter day. "For me," he began, "the kingdom of God is perfection in all seasons." Clearly, his choice showed perfection in the season of winter. But his words added a blanket of deeper meaning that God can be perfectly present to us in all seasons—even in winter. That is what Sarah needed to hear: that even in this season of despair, there was permission to dwell in that season and even somehow to discover perfection in her grief there.

Not only is there perfection in all seasons, but there is also perfection in all voices coming together. Our hallelujahs might be discordant, our minor keys might be harder to perfect their pitch, our souls might not even feel like joining in, but somehow still the song goes on and perfection is found in its singing. Even in our offkeyness there is perfection for God. Even in our brokenness, God is filled with joy by our singing praise. Perhaps it is our brokenness that assigns different notes and eventually offers fullness in sound. Even when there doesn't seem to be a "hallelujah" left in us, there is still something about this word that echoes, as Howard Rice says, "the language of the soul"[2]—even when we feel soulless. Simply saying "praise the Lord" doesn't fulfill the same need. The guttural utterance of those long-spoken syllables, "hallelujah," is what our souls need.

The word "hallelujah" literally means "Let us praise Yahweh." It occurs only in Psalms 104 through 150 and briefly in Revelation 19:1–8. Though used only in that span of Psalms, it is used often in the beginning and end of a psalm to lead the reader into tune. Now the word echoes on through the Psalms, through the underpeals and many waters of Revelation, through the centuries of medieval plainsong and Handel's "Hallelujah Chorus" to this day, when its recitation is still an important part of our worship. Even when we can't imagine singing a "hallelujah" in God's angel chorus, something within us still primitively utters this language of the soul.

No one knew this better than David himself. A composer of psalms and poems, his legacy sings on loudly. His life was discordant—the entanglement with Bathsheba, the abuse of power, the disconnect with his sons, and yet he knew the major lifts of the grace of God. It was with the acknowledgment of all this that he—though baffled by it at times—still sang out "hallelujah." His hallelujah wasn't an arrival of pure faith or a dismissal of all the pain; his hallelujah was a yearning, an entreaty in itself. He knew there would be a day for a whole and flawless hallelujah. But for now there was just his baffled voice.

Perhaps David was baffled because he knew that the majors and the minors are reconfigured in God's song; that sometimes in the story of God sung out in the world it is the minors that are lifted and the majors that are fallen. Perhaps he was baffled because he knew too that sometimes as we stand before God singing, our priorities are rebalanced.

What were minor worries and insecurities fall away in view of what is most major and praiseworthy and laudable in the sight of God.

Isn't that precisely what singing praise is all about? By the very nature of ascribing praise to some things, we are declaring other things in our lives and in the world as unworthy of praise. By lifting up the praiseworthy, the major and the minor are reconfigured. This is the song that is sung for us. It surely provides comfort for those in the dark.

I worked with a youth group who loved to sing. In the church vans, around the table, late at night, early in the morning, in the airport, in worship and in fellowship, their identity was shaped by song. Pleasing not only to God but to all who heard their voices, they could sing the sweetest hallelujah I have ever heard. One of their spine-tingling, poignant, awe-inspiring songs was called "Hope for Resolution." It combined the classic "Of the Father's Love Begotten" with a South African freedom song from the days of apartheid. The piece began hauntingly with the ancient plainsong intonations written by Aurelius Clemens Prudentius in the fourth century. Then suddenly, the freedom song broke out. The piece concluded with a weaving together of these two sung prayers.

On one youth retreat we met a man from South Africa named Spiwo. During sermons throughout a weeklong conference we heard his tales of struggle in South Africa. In and out of jail for resisting oppression, there were times when his ability to sing the songs of his faith and the songs that prayed for freedom were limited by jailers and prison rules. At the end of the conference a member from our group invited him for dinner and discussion. At the end of the evening the group asked if they could share a song with him. They began, "Of the Father's love begotten, ere the world began to be, he is Alpha and Omega, he the source, the ending he." When the rhythm changed and they broke out into Swahili, singing the freedom song, tears began to stream down his face. "You know my song!" he cried out. When the piece was over, he expressed his thanks. "You don't know what it means to me," he explained, "to know that people around the world were singing our song of freedom when we didn't always have the freedom or the courage to sing it ourselves. Your singing denounced intolerance and injustice when we were unable to sing it ourselves. Thanks for keeping the song going for me."

Though the bafflement and the imperfection are there now, one day we will stand before God and the perfection and understanding will be complete. Until then, we just have to keep the song going for those who can't sing—but even more so, to bring joy to the Lord of song who longs for our praise and our singing. Our songs are raised as armor and amulets, blessings and triumphs, doors flung open, and comfort in the dark.

Offering

The only thing I regret is my economies.

—Reynolds Price

*O*ne of the greatest scenes in movie history is Oskar Schindler holding his cufflinks in his hand at the end of *Schindler's List*. The movie portrays Schindler, a member of the Nazi Party, working against the government as he buys Jews to put them to work in a weapons factory. His secret is that the weapons factory is making worthless weapons. His purchase of Jews is an attempt at salvation in the midst of the horrors of anti-Semitism. As the movie comes to an end, scenes of offering unfold. In case the Allies caught him, the leaders of the Jewish community write a letter explaining the good deeds Schindler had done. The Jewish workers line up one by one to have gold from their teeth extracted to make a ring for Schindler. Inscribed inside the ring are the words from the Talmud, "Whoever saves one life, saves the world entire."

The offerings continue. Schindler makes sure that each of the Jews receives vodka and cigarettes, not to be consumed, but to be used for trade. He knows these items could be the difference between life and death for them as they journey home. But the real difference between life and death becomes most apparent to Schindler as he looks at the clothes he is wearing. "I threw away so much money," he laments. "If I had just. . . ." One of the Jewish leaders interrupts him: "There will be generations because of what you have done." Schindler continues as he regrets his economies: "I didn't do enough. This car, this could have saved ten people. This pin, it could have saved two people. This cufflink, one more person, one more person could be standing here for this. I could've saved one more person and I didn't."

We Christians would do well to look at our cufflinks. It is ironic to me that so much of the Bible is devoted to issues of stewardship—tithing and wealth, jubilee offerings and the yield of one's harvest—and yet we spend so little time internalizing what this means for our lives. Over and over again the message is clear: "Share the wealth." Still we continue, as one pastor put it, "to spend more each month on our gas and pizza bill than we give to the church."

Ten percent. Who wants to hear that at stewardship season? We tip-toe around the issue, hiring consultants, coming up with theme verses, putting offering plates in the back of the sanctuary and allowing the desires of a congregation not to hear about money dictate the message of the stewardship sermon. We want to know what the church offers us rather than wrestle with what cufflinks we need to pull out of our drawers and offer the church. Michael Lindvall tells of his words to new member classes: "You have a right to ask what this church can offer you. But there is another question you ought to ask. And it's not the second question, but the first. You need to ask what you can offer the church."[1]

We are quick to determine other ways of giving that sidestep the church. Many a pastor has heard the question, "Why should I give to the church when I could put this money directly in the pocket of someone who needs it and minimize the administrative costs?" This question assumes the wrong thing. We do not give *to* the church; we give *as* a church. We give as a body of people, who discern the needs of our community and world, and give in the name of Jesus Christ. Of course some of that money supports a building and a staff, but both are necessary in proclaiming the gospel. Our giving to the church should not be out of guilt or shame, but in response to our own internalization of the gospel and its demand on our lives.

Christ honors the one woman in the Bible who put in her two cents. She recognized Christ and knew his claim on her life. He goes on to say, "Truly I tell you, this poor widow has put in more than all of them; for all of them have contributed out of their abundance, but she out of her poverty has put in all she had to live on" (Mark 12:43–44).

Her offering was a matter of life and death. She gave everything that she had to live on. In so doing, her offering demanded her trust in a God who would provide. In a sermon preached by Dave Davis, he referred to the "Clink, clink" of the widow's offering. The echo of those two copper coins continues to this day and challenges us to ask ourselves, "Are we willing to put in all that we have to live on?" In our holding on to our coins, to our cufflinks, to our gas and pizza bill, we economize, and thereby strangle the message of the gospel. It is hard to imagine a stewardship campaign being led by the words "Your Offering Is a Matter of Life and Death." Although the fact is clear, its truth is hard to hear.

Rainer Maria Rilke writes, "The transformed speaks only to relinquishers / All holders-on are stranglers."[2] We are able to relinquish because we are transformed. We are able to let go because we are held on to. Our offering is about what we let go of; it is about much more than our money. It is relinquishing control and fear, because we know that in the relinquishing, God transforms them. The act of offering is letting go of desire and want. It is allowing ourselves to be vulnerable and unsure of what the future will bring. To relinquish is to save a life; to hold on is to choose death. Our offering is truly a matter of life and death.

Two recent college graduates I know were confronted with the need of a homeless family in Appalachia. Because their student loans totaled more than $100,000, they lived on the salary of the teacher in the family and used the salary of the other to pay off the loans. Learning of three children who did not have a roof over their heads, they sent a check for a thousand dollars immediately. "What's another month of paying off this loan for us when their need is for today?" They knew that lives were at stake and their faith necessitated that they choose life.

The needs of the day are not just financial. We can offer ourselves above and beyond our wallets to the needs of this world. An artist seeing children bored after school in a lower-income neighborhood near her home in Virginia loads up her station wagon with art supplies and operates a community art center from the trunk of her car. A seminarian confronted with a man on death row who claims his innocence quits school, learns the law and devotes his life to freeing those wrongly convicted. A corporate executive from California learns the needs of an orphanage in Washington, D.C., quits her job, sells her home, packs her bags and shows up to become a dorm mother. "Now there is never a day I don't want to wake up. How could I miss seeing the smile on one of the kids' faces?" Relinquishing norms, expectations and fears, these faithful find freedom in letting go of the gravity holding them in their place and in turn acknowledge that they are held by grace.

In the movie *Jerry Maguire*, Tom Cruise plays a sports agent who has become numb to the effects of his career choices. As the film begins, Cruise visits a client of his who is in the hospital due to head and neck injuries. Devoted to football and lured by its financial possibilities, his client refuses to stop playing the game even though it is clear the game is wreaking havoc on his body. In a halfhearted attempt to reassure his client's young son, Cruise throws empty words of reassurance his way. In anger, the young boy tells Cruise exactly what he thinks of his life's work. In that moment, Cruise is struck by the shallow and meaningless offering of his life.

The confrontation with the child causes Cruise to reevaluate everything. Late that night he begins writing a mission statement to propose a new way of living and working. As he types page after page in a manic moment of self-evaluation, he hears the words "Suddenly I was my father's son again." For Cruise, this revelation is a reminder of whose he is. He becomes further aware of the stagnancy of his life thus far, and hopeful of a new stage of generativity that might be life-giving both to him and to his clients.

Erik Erikson writes that one of the critical stages of our development comes as we are faced with the challenge of stagnancy versus generativity.[3] For Erikson, generativity is "the concern for establishing and guiding the next generation." This concern is not just about having and raising children; it is the power of productivity and creativity to be life-giving to others. Our offering has the potential to generate beyond ourselves, over and above ourselves, into the kingdom of God. Generations might be saved because of our offering. In contrast, Erikson explains, a pervading sense of stagnation develops out of boredom, interpersonal impoverishment and especially an obsession with our own needs. In other words, our economizing in a vain attempt to hold on strangles and stagnates our lives. Death is the only result. We may not see the immediate results of our economies, but the kingdom of God knows them.

God calls us to a new economy, one that offers both time and talents. Time, without an offering of money, is devoid of the full sacrifice that God challenges us to. Money, without time shared in risk and relationship, is devoid of the fullness of the community God intends. Those who reason with themselves during stewardship season simply to offer more of their time rather than more of their money minimize the gospel message. Anyone who writes a check without knowing a name and a face misses the kingdom of God.

God's economy looks completely different from any economic system we have lived under. It's an economic system where there are no regrets for what we've given, all are paid the same wage, the last become first and the first become last. God's economy generates a kingdom that is bigger than our fears, broader than our desires, wider than our attempts to economize. In God's economic system, two copper coins are the epitome of abundance; cufflinks, a matter of life and death. Offering as an act of worship demands that we become our Father's children again. In so doing, we trust in a new way, offer our lives in a wholly new way. We let go of our cufflinks and coins, loan payments and educational goals. We lose our lives, so that others might be saved. In our relinquishing, lives are saved, generations will grow.

Prayers of the People

Something opens our wings. Something
makes boredom and hurt disappear.
Someone fills the cup in front of us.
We taste only sacredness.
                    —Rumi, "Something Opens Our Wings"[1]

*W*hy is it that prayer can be so difficult to sip? A taste of sacredness
sits before us, and we close our mouths. Why is it hard to open them?
To offer up hurts so that they might disappear? To turn from our boredom toward a more satisfying existence? We Presbyterians are often
reluctant to pray out loud. Give us a list of prayer concerns, a litany
of prayer or a phone chain, and we are much more comfortable. But
the one-on-one, hand-in-hand kind of prayer, for either pastor or
layperson, can be tough. Even when we have the words—a psalm, the
Lord's Prayer—it still can be hard to pray. We close our mouths, shy
away, feel like we have no words, retreat within ourselves to a personal one-on-one conversation with God alone.

But then something happens. Rumi describes the unclinching and
the unfolding. Our mouths open to take a sip; our wings unfold and
prayer takes flight. That something is indescribable until you have
experienced it. Desperation comes close to describing it. But even as
cares and worry weigh down the heart and mind, prayer grows the
wings of vulnerability and intimacy and takes flight.

Nehemiah knew both the taste and flight of prayer. He lived after
the exile and the return to Jerusalem. The first chapter opens with his

grievous lament over the destruction of Jerusalem and his call to begin rebuilding the walls of the city. What we know about this man Nehemiah is fragmentary, but these pieces alone are as strong as the wall he helped to build. With unskilled labor and despite intense opposition, he directed the completion of the wall of Jerusalem. Before being appointed governor of Judah, his day-to-day job was that of cupbearer to the king, a job that daily faced life or death as he tasted every sip of the king's cup to ensure that it was not poisoned. If it was poisoned, Nehemiah, fatally, would be the first to find out. As a cupbearer, Nehemiah had access to the inner court and access to the throne itself. There he probably heard a lot and talked very little. Though his position was highly respected, it still was a position of humility. Perhaps the closest thing today to being a cupbearer to the king would be serving as a Secret Service agent. Yet the amazing thing about Nehemiah's life isn't that he rebuilt the wall of Jerusalem, or the responsibility he faced each day; it is the taste of his prayer life that fills our cup as well.

In Sunday school, years ago, Mrs. Moore taught us a simple acronym about prayer. "Don't know how to pray?" she said. "Try this: P-R-A-Y. Praise, Remember, Ask, Yield." She went on to explain how we should praise God for all God's wonderful gifts and attributes. We should remember in confession what we have done, and remember in Scripture how God is faithful. Then we should ask God for whatever our need or the need of the world, and finally yield to God in acknowledgment that God has plans bigger and wiser than our plans. In yielding we affirm just what Voltaire penned: "The only fitting prayer is an act of submission." I still use her acronym to this day if I am at a loss for prayer.

Nehemiah's prayer follows the same pattern (Neh. 1:5–11). He praises "the Lord God of heaven, the great and awesome God who keeps covenant and steadfast love with those who love him and keep his commandments." He remembers the sins of his people, his own sins and the sins of his family. Then he remembers words spoken to Moses: "If you are unfaithful, I will scatter you among the peoples; but if you return to me and keep my commandments I will gather them." What he asks of God is bold. Nehemiah asks for success and mercy as he approaches the throne of the king to ask permission to work on the wall of Jerusalem. Then he yields.

It is his position as cupbearer that gives Nehemiah access to the king and enables him to make such a bold request. In the midst of the huge responsibility of being cupbearer, Nehemiah realized that his responsibility held a possibility. He had access to the throne. But it wasn't just in his public position that Nehemiah had access to the throne; it is also in his life of prayer where Nehemiah found access to the throne of grace. The life of a cupbearer and the life of prayer sound pretty similar to me—a position with access to the throne of grace, a position where you talk little but hear a lot, a position of humility and yet of tremendous respect, a position that is a matter of life and death.

What I learn from Nehemiah is that I too can approach the throne of grace. Bearing all the responsibilities of my life, bearing all the prayers spoken and unspoken, with my cup as full as it can possibly be some days, and at other times empty and dry, I set it there on the throne of grace at the foot of the King. Some days I set the cup there gracefully; other days it spills out. For me bearing the cup is a way of giving voice to exactly where I am at—in the midst of all my responsibilities, insecurities, questions and insistent petitions. It's a way of spilling out all these things and a way of being filled up anew. Once I've spilled it out in prayer, I drink up God's refreshing words of hope and grace.

We spill out and drink up because we know the woe and suffering of the world. The language of the cup is not unique to Nehemiah. The psalmist used the image of the cup to speak to both the joy and the pain of life. From the comforting words of Psalm 23, "my cup overflows" (23:5), implying an abundance of goodness and mercy, to the anguish of Psalm 11, "a scorching wind shall be their cup" (11:6), we know the taste of life in between these two glasses. Psalm 116:13 calls it the cup of salvation; the Suffering Servant (Isa. 51:17) knows it as the cup of God's wrath. Our prayers lap up everything in between. We know wrath and salvation. We know the thirst that comes from the hesitancy to drink from either cup.

We search for successful ways to pray because we are thirsty for God's response. I think that thirst comes not from wanting God's perfect answer, but from desiring God's personal interaction. We long for the revelation of God's hand in the outpouring of our days. Yet while the search presupposes an openness to God's hand, sometimes the search becomes an excuse for not being open to God's hand. We don't want to open ourselves to God because that means having to empty ourselves of what has filled that unclaimed space.

Sometimes in my prayer life I am acutely aware of a resistance. It is an absolute unwillingness to pour out my inner thoughts to God. I want to hold on to the pain or the petition at all costs because it fills a void. To name that prayer, to let it go, means facing the unknown and needing something new to hold on to, and I don't always have the courage or the will to do that. It would mean relying on God's grace instead of my own grasp.

The story of the fisher king has been told over and over again. The tale begins when the king is a boy. He is sent out to spend the night in the forest to prove his courage so he can be king. While he is there, he sees a sacred vision, a fiery vision—and in the midst of the fire is the Holy Grail, a symbol to him of God's divine grace. The boy hears a voice: "You shall be keeper of the grail, so that it may heal the hearts of humankind." But the boy is blinded by greater visions—the grasp of power and glory and strength. For a moment he feels invincible and not dependent on anyone but himself, and as he reached for the grail, it vanishes and the fire burns his hand.

As the boy grew older, the wound grew deeper. Life began to lose its meaning and its reason. He had no faith in anyone, not another person, not God, not himself. He couldn't love nor could he be loved. He was ready to die. When he wasn't thinking about death, he was thinking about the grail and how he let it slip away.

One day a fool wandered into his castle. Being of different mind than most, the fool didn't see a king, but a man alone and in pain. The fool asked, "What ails you friend?" And the king said, "I am thirsty." So the fool took the cup beside the bed of the king and filled it with water and handed it to the king. As the king began to drink, he realized that his wound was healed. When he looked into his hands, there was the Holy Grail, that divine grace he had sought all his life. The king turned to the fool and asked, "How could you find that which I have searched for all my life?" The fool replied, "I don't know. I only knew that you were thirsty."

There is something about the life of prayer that demands our foolishness and our naïveté. Even more so, it demands an honest recognition of the needs of our brothers and sisters. Our life of prayer calls for us to be willing to bear the cup for others who are thirsty, who need a nourishing sip of divine grace. But instead of playing the fool, I am much more likely to play the role of the king, thirsty and searching, stubborn and grasping. Yet it is the fool in all his foolishness that provides comfort through his simple action of bearing the cup.

When I feel resistant to spilling out and instead find myself desperately grasping hold of control, I try and remember a spiritual I learned in worship. While singing the words, worshipers sat with hands unfolded, cupped like wings, and lifted, preparing to hear the Word of God. We sang,

> Here's my cup Lord, I lift it up Lord.
> Come and fill this yearning in my soul.
> Water of life, nourish me till I want no more.
> Here's my cup, fill it up, and make me whole.

Nehemiah knows what it means to bear the cup. He knows firsthand that it is a matter of life and death. But he also knows the comfort found in bearing the cup to God in a life of prayer. His name means in Hebrew "Yahweh comforts." What I love about his name is that it does not mean "God fixes everything" or "God can meet your every wish and desire" or "God makes your life happy and perfect." His name instead is a true testament to prayer, that there is something about a life of prayer that brings reassurance. When we bear our cups to the throne of grace, whether we come spilling all over the place or empty and dry, we find comfort.

A family I know has been going through a very uncomfortable time. Facing cancer and the loss of a job and then bearing the responsibility of talking to their children about the convergence of both has been a crisis. When their daughter heard the news, she talked to God about her feelings. In the midst of prayer, she had a revelation: We can make a quilt, a comforter of sorts.

So she and her sisters began picking out fabric, cutting out pieces and stitching up their pain and fear. They hid it in the basement of their grandparents' home for weeks on end. The design was a pattern of hearts, a simple testament of love and comfort for their mom and dad. The answer to their prayer was simple. Their parents needed love and comfort, and the girls knew just how to make that happen.

The Directory for Worship of the Presbyterian Church (U.S.A.) avows, "Prayer is at the heart of worship." And at that heart is a God who provides incredible comfort. The directory goes on to say,

> In prayer we respond to God in many ways. In adoration we praise God for who God is. In thanksgiving we express gratitude for what God has done. In confession we acknowledge repentance for what we as individuals and as a people have done or left undone. In supplication we plead for ourselves and the gathered community. In intercession we plead for others, on behalf of others, and for the whole world. In self-dedication we offer ourselves to the purpose and glory of God.[2]

To me that call sounds like bearing the cup. Prayer is about approaching the throne of grace with humility and respect. Prayer is a place where you talk little and listen much. Prayer is a place of access to the King. Prayer is a place that is ultimately a matter of life and death.

Christ himself knew the demand of bearing the cup. The cup contained joy and salvation, woe and suffering. Christ's cup was filled with the prayers of all people. It was also filled with his own: "Abba, Father, for you all things are possible; remove this cup from me; yet, not what I want, but what you want" (Mark 14:36). His prayer praised, remembered and asked. He knew his position as cupbearer for the world was a matter of life and death. But he also knew that, ultimately, bearing the cup in prayer was about yielding to God, and so he did. His yielding is what makes our boredom and our hurt disappear, because he is the one who fills the cup in front of us.

The Lord's Prayer

When I pray, I enter into the depth of my own heart and find there the heart of God, who speaks to me of love. And I recognize, right there, the place where all of my sisters and brothers are in communion with one another. The great paradox of the spiritual life is, indeed, that the most personal is most universal, that the most intimate, is most communal.
—*Henri J. Nouwen,* Here and Now[1]

*D*uring seminary I served as a student intern in the chaplain's office of the local hospital. Every week, each of the interns spent one evening on call. We would sleep in the psychiatric unit of the hospital with beeper in hand, ready to respond to any call. The first night, the beeper went off at 11:00 p.m. I called the number and at the other end of the line was a young woman who lived far away. Her grandfather was in the hospital in the intensive care unit. He had left the church, she explained, but she wondered if I would be willing to go up and see him anyway. She was concerned about him being alone. So I went up.

I entered his room, introduced myself and told him about the phone call from his granddaughter. He smiled. Unable to speak because of the tracheotomy tube in his throat, he picked up a pen and pad. Trying to decipher his message was difficult: letters were missing, backwards and overlapping. After some time, his request became clear. He was asking for the Lord's Prayer.

I grabbed his hand and said the Lord's Prayer, slowly and clearly. "Our Father . . . who art in heaven. . . ." When I was done, he began to write once again. And again after a time of deciphering, I understood his request. Pray it again, louder this time. "OUR FATHER, WHO ART IN HEAVEN . . . ," I prayed, as I had many times before.

Once again he took the pad in hand and asked if I would say the prayer again, this time saying, "*My* father. . . ." Wanting the prayer to be just perfect for him, I complied. Loud and clear, slow and deliberate, personalizing it just for him I began, "*MY* FATHER, WHO ART IN HEAVEN. . . ."

Then I forgot every single word of the Lord's Prayer. It was one of those moments seminary can never prepare you for. One of those times you think will never happen because you have prayed that prayer so many times before. The words were as familiar as my best friend, and yet in the midst of praying, I forgot every single word I ever knew. Bread, I said to myself, it has something to do with bread. And temptation too. I scanned the childhood recesses of my brain; I revisited Sunday school with Mrs. Farris; I tried sitting in chapel and praying as I always had. But no words came to mind. I was sweating my prayer. Mentors have advised, always have a copy of the Lord's Prayer and the Apostles' Creed with you. Keep on you the 23rd Psalm. Carry the Bible and the printed prayers with you. You will need them. And I certainly did.

I sat there holding his hand and feeling a great responsibility. Would I fail him as the church had before? When the disciples explained to Jesus that sometimes they just did not know what to pray, Christ taught them the Lord's Prayer. But what do you do when you can't even remember that?

The answer is in Christ's word to his disciples. In Matthew he says, "When you are praying, do not heap up empty phrases as the Gentiles do; for they think that they will be heard because of their many words" (Matt. 6:7). We are raised to believe that prayer is about words and phrases. We recite the Lord's Prayer, read the prayer of confession, offer up litanies and collects. Even with the most devout of hearts, these prayers can become empty phrases—even the one Jesus himself taught us.

Prayer becomes empty when we forget that what is most important about prayer is the relationship—the relationship between ourselves and God. As Nouwen describes, "When I pray, I enter into the depth of my own heart and find there the heart of God, who speaks to me of love." He goes on to describe how the relationship becomes even deeper: "and I recognize, right there, the place where all of my sisters and brothers are in communion with one another. The great paradox of the spiritual life is, indeed, that the most personal is most universal, that the most intimate, is most communal." Here we see that at the heart of prayer is a relationship that extends beyond the vertical toward God, to the horizontal embrace of our brothers and sisters.

Prayer as relationship extends in another dimension as well. Prayer calls on us to relate imaginatively to both the petitions we recite and the petitions that rise up from our hearts. If we are praying the Lord's Prayer asking God to "give us this day our daily bread," we lose the fullness of the prayer if our minds focus on bread alone. This petition invites us to pray for the nourishment of all God's children. In a time of war, we pray for those whose daily bread are rations or Meals Ready to Eat. In a time of peace, we might pray for those who are hungry due to the misdistribution of resources. The petition also lifts up those who need living bread, the spiritual sustenance that only Christ can provide. When we leave our imaginations at the door of the sanctuary, when we forget the breadth this prayer calls us to as we say it with our children each night, we neglect the many dimensions of the relationship of prayer. This prayer is not just about our intimate relationship with God; it is about our communal relationships with all of God's creation. Still, it's so easy at times just to say the words.

A friend explained it to me this way: "At age 32, I couldn't tell you the last time I actually thought about what each petition of the Lord's Prayer actually means; I've just said it." She went on to describe how her seven-year-old daughter, Courtney, was learning the lines of the Lord's Prayer in Sunday school. Working through each petition week to week, she missed a few weeks when her grandfather became sick. Back in Sunday school, she was asked to draw a picture of "thy kingdom come, thy will be done." She drew a breathtaking picture of flowers, clouds and the sky opening up to heaven. Weeks later, the young girl's grandfather died and the picture became a prayer for them of his presence in heaven. The picture now is framed and in the hallway for all to see each day. Courtney explained its presence as a prayer for understanding. The picture doesn't just give hope about all being together one day—it calls Courtney to a new relationship. In it she envisions the prayer anew each time she prays it so that it will be empty no longer.

A participant in a class on worship offered these words to further develop each line of the prayer: "Our Father who art in heaven—*Relationship*, Hallowed be thy name—*Revere*, Thy kingdom come—*Renew*, Thy will be done—*Reveal*, On earth as it is in heaven—*Reconcile*, Give us this day our daily bread—*Replenish*, And forgive us our debts—*Remove*, As we forgive our debtors—*Relinquish*, And lead us not into temptation—*Reject*, But deliver us from evil—*Redirect*, For thine is the kingdom—*Recognize*, And the power—*Respect*, And the glory—*Resurrect*, Forever—*Remember*. Amen."

Praying with the man in ICU, I didn't need words to a prayer. What mattered was the relationship—my hand holding this man's, God's hand upholding us both. There are no perfect prayers, but there are empty words. What matters is purity of heart and integrity of spirit. The patient and I were in communion with God that night; the room was alive with the Spirit of God poured out upon us. The prayer I whispered in my own heart after forgetting the words was a prayer of relationship and respect, reverence and renewal. All of the components of the Lord's Prayer were there, just not the exact phrasing.

A young confirmand struggled in class with her desire to pray in worship; she felt like the words and phrases had become empty. "I don't just want to go through the motions," she said. It was clear these words were a prayer for integrity both in the sanctuary and outside the sanctuary as well. She wanted to live a life that had meaning and purpose. Her questions and struggles enhanced the confirmation experience of everyone in the class. Her honesty provoked others to do the same, and her answers brought wisdom. One day after the previous week's discussion on prayer, she came with copies of the following prayer. "I brought this so we could all think about what it really means and not just say it," she said. The words practically danced off the page with the movement of the spirit within her. All prayed with a renewed sense of the relationship of words to image, ourselves to God, as we said the following together:

Our Father
  A real person who cares for and loves me,
Who art in heaven
  Living higher than I am, understanding more than I,
Hallowed be thy name
  We honor and praise your holy name,
Thy kingdom come
  Yes, come quickly, Lord Jesus, come into our lives,
Thy will be done
  You always know what is best for us,
On earth as it is in heaven
  As you always have and always will,
Give us this day our daily bread
  You have always supplied our needs,
And forgive us our debts
  In the name of Christ,
As we forgive our debtors
  Seventy times seven, Lord,
And lead us not into temptation
  Give us the strength to resist,
But deliver us from evil
  When we fall, you come through,
For thine is the kingdom
  In which we share,
And the power
  Greater than anything we have ever known,
And the glory forever,
  Which we see revealed everywhere.
Amen.

Though this prayer was written years ago by young Mary, I recently closed a session on a mission trip with it. I was with a group of middle-school youth in Hollywood, California. A bona fide Hollywood producer and Presbyterian came to meet with our eager group. He is the producer of *X2,* and if you have seen the movie, you know it highlights the Lord's Prayer. Nightcrawler, a character in the movie, looks devilish at first sight, but it is slowly revealed that he is a very faithful creature. Proving that Christians aren't always what you might expect them to look like, Nightcrawler summons strength for himself and others in the movie through his faithful actions. At one critical scene, he begins saying the Lord's Prayer. Hearing the depth of his voice, one is clear that the prayer is more than just words to him. Each petition has meaning and salvation for him as he quietly says them and others learn from his devotion.

Our group listened intently as we heard about the producer's involvement in the faithful elements of the movie. When we were finished, we closed with this version of the Lord's Prayer written by the fourteen-year-old girl. "Could I have a copy of that?" the producer asked. I love to think that he related to this prayer in a new way that day. Maybe somewhere in his Hollywood office his eyes catch sight of her words intertwined with the words of our Lord Jesus Christ, who taught us what to pray so our words won't be empty, nor will the relationships of our lives.

There can be comfort in the repetition of the Lord's Prayer each week in worship, even each day at home. The man in the hospital requested the prayer because he knew the comfort those petitions bring. They bring comfort when relationships are remembered. Relationships call to mind particular pictures and memories; so too does this prayer when prayed with a sense of the imagination, a remembrance of the communal and a desire to have an intimate relationship with God.

Sealing

Sealing

Signed, sealed, delivered . . . I'm yours

—Stevie Wonder

*I*f you've heard Stevie Wonder's old hit "Signed, Sealed, Delivered . . . I'm Yours," then you know it is a soul-filled song about a love letter. If you've checked your e-mail account lately, then you also know that letter writing is a lost art. In this Internet day and age, there is nothing better than intimate words handwritten, a name inscribed in real ink and the joy of a real letter sent to your mailbox. I received a great love letter for Mother's Day this year. The words were Hallmark's, not my husband's, but the thought was perfect. "In the beginning," it said, "God created the world and populated it with children. They were cute and wonderful, but they made a mess. God added some animals, all sorts of them, but things got even messier. God created the first dad, Adam, and then, well, then the world REALLY became a mess. So then, God created moms." I told him to buy fifty and save them for the next five decades of life together.

Stevie Wonder was singing about love letters. But what he didn't realize was that he was also singing about the sacraments—baptism and Communion. His words, though unintentional, make a theological statement and sum up succinctly exactly what baptism and Communion are all about. The Directory for Worship states, "Sacraments are *signs* of the real presence and power of Christ in the Church, symbols of God's action. Through the Sacraments, God *seals* believers in redemption, renews their identity as the people of God, and marks

115

them for service."[1] In other words, the sacraments are signs of God's invisible love and grace. They seal upon our hearts the Holy Spirit. They deliver us from evil and back into the embrace of God. Stevie Wonder may not have realized it, but his words aren't just about letters of love—these words can be about bread broken, wine poured, the waters of baptism and a promise kept. It is the promises made here in the sacrament that claim us: "I am yours, God," we say in baptism and Communion. And God says to us the very same.

I remember the first time I heard the oft-quoted phrase of St. Augustine "The sacraments are visible signs of God's invisible love and grace." It was midway through a tough year teaching confirmation class. Forty youth meeting regularly on Sunday mornings throughout the year were a little hard to keep awake without massive amounts of donuts and coffee. Make the teenagers excited about the gospel and church membership? We had ideas and lesson plans. We prayed and hoped. But still we needed a full-blown movement of the Holy Spirit.

Sneaking into the sanctuary in the few quiet moments between the two worship services, we found it surprisingly dark and almost eerie. We stood huddled around the Communion table. In a sanctuary large enough to seat hundreds, standing so close to the table seemed sacrilegious. There was a reverence and silence there that day normally reserved for serious things, like the principal's office. Then the pastor took the bread and wine, set and ready there for the Communion yet to come, and whispered, "These are visible signs of God's invisible love and grace." There could have been countless lesson plans eliciting the importance of the sacraments and the history and theology of their enactment. But in that quiet whisper, we all witnessed that love made visible.

Stevie Wonder didn't know the full power of his words when he talked about a love letter being "signed and sealed." It was the power of the Holy Spirit that sealed that understanding upon our hearts in the whisper "These are visible signs of God's invisible love and grace." That is where this idea of "sealing" comes in. Sacraments seal the Holy Spirit upon our hearts. Words might have a lick and a kiss, but without the Holy Spirit, nothing is going to stick, let alone be sealed.

In the Presbyterian tradition, "sealing" is separated as a particular movement in worship. The language of "sealing" is unique to our order of service. Some traditions, following the Fourfold Rite of the Wester Ordo, honor "The Meal" as the third full movement of worship. Other traditions compress the sacraments into the act of "responding." Theologically this is troubling when it is clear that the sacraments are all about God's gracious response to us—no matter what. The sacraments of baptism and Communion are acts separate from our "responding" to the proclamation of the gospel. These acts are God's gracious initiative to us so that the Spirit might be sealed upon our hearts.

The language of sealing comes from the wonderful seals of Old Testament times. Kings had fancy rings fashioned with elaborate designs for the sealing of documents. Without the wax and the impression of the ring, no contract was complete, no letter was official. Documents depended on these impressions for their validity. These seals were devices that designated ownership. Seals provided identification of the sender and prestige to those who received them. Some seals were cylindrical in shape; when rolled into wax, or sometimes clay, a picture or inscription was revealed. Often these pictures were theological in nature.

In Isaiah 29:11–14 the prophet tells the people of Israel that they are looking at the wrong picture.

> The vision of the Lord has become for you like the words of a sealed document. It is given to those who can read, with the command, "Read this," they say, "We cannot, for it is sealed." And if it is given to those who cannot read, saying, "Read this," they say, "We cannot read." The Lord said: Because people draw near with their mouths and honor me with their lips, while their hearts are far from me, and their worship of me is a human commandment learned by rote; so I will again do amazing things with this people, shocking and amazing. The wisdom of their wise shall perish, and the discernment of the discerning shall be hidden.

The people of Israel have been making excuse after excuse, saying they cannot see the words God has put into their hands. Perhaps the Word of God is even closer than the words of the document; perhaps the Word of God is evident in the picture embossed into the seal of the document. There in that seal they might just see a visible sign of the invisible love and grace of God. Perhaps if they look more closely, instead of making excuses, they might see God's Word revealed. Isaiah uses this image of a seal to describe how we sometimes look for God in the wrong places. Instead of seeing what is in front of our very own eyes, we look to other places. While the other places might remind us of where we have seen God's presence in the past, by neglecting what is in front of us we miss seeing God's hand in the present moment.

Perhaps the vision of the Lord is even closer than in the words written in that sealed document. Maybe God's vision is rolled out in a picture captured in the wax used to seal the document. If the people have the eyes to look in an unexpected place, they might just see shocking and amazing things. We look to numbers or the bottom line or total agreement on a tough issue to see a picture of God rolled out as we want to see it, when maybe the picture that needs to be seen is the impact on an individual, not numbers. Or perhaps it is in working through the disagreement. We look for perfection and order and legibility, and yet God does not always speak that way.

Isaiah is speaking to a people who were looking for God in the wrong places. God's vision, he says, has become for you like the words of a sealed document. In other words, you want to read what is written inside, when maybe, just maybe, God is giving you something to look at—a picture sealed into the wax on the outside of the letter—that might just be closer than you think.

In a church in New Jersey years ago, midway through the celebration of Communion, it became clear to all that there was not enough bread and wine for everyone to receive some. The congregation became antsy. How would this be solved? Aren't we as Presbyterians supposed to do this decently and in order? Who was responsible for buying enough for everyone? What happened to the planning?

A few elders departed from the back of the sanctuary. The pastor announced they were going grocery shopping and until all had received the elements, we would sing hymns together as a church. We began to sing. Some members looked at their watches and, seeing that noon was coming quickly, went out the back doors. They were the ones looking for God in the wrong places. I've been there before, sneaking out the back door. Have you? Instead of seeing a beautiful picture of the real meaning of Communion rolled out into the waxy seal of life, some were looking instead for God's writing in the document.

We look for God in the wrong places, ignoring the seal on the envelope, when we want life to run perfectly, everything decent and in order. Maybe the very picture God is calling us to see is this picture rolled out into the waxy mess of not quite enough elements. Once this picture is seen, then the waiting takes on new meaning because it shows a whole new understanding of Communion. This Communion would not be complete until all had participated; not one person would be left out. God rolls out images for us to see of God's kingdom here on earth. Do we have eyes to see the pictures on these seals? Isaiah tells us, if we have eyes to see them, they are shocking and amazing. If we do not have eyes to see them, our lives and our worship become rote.

In the sacraments, we are invited to see these shocking and amazing pictures of God rolled out into the wax and the clay of our everyday lives. The pictures reveal a God who takes delight in the washing of an infant, joy in the bathing of an adult. The pictures reveal a God who sits down at the table with us and invites us to partake of the feast. These pictures are rolled out over and over again in worship—stamped into the wax of our ways—because so much of that wax can be chipped away in the everydayness of our lives. We forget who we are and whose we are. "Have you forgotten?" God asks. "Are you feeling a little worn and chipped?" Without even an answer, God rolls out the picture again. "Remember it looks like this—you are my child at any age. And don't forget it tastes like this, a little crumbly and bitter—but sweet and satisfying at the same time."

Once, discussing these pictures of God seen in the sacraments, I invited a group to describe where they see these pictures—these promises of God made in baptism and Communion—in their day-to-day life. "I'm not sure I see these in my daily life," Marti offered. "These are corporate, not individual, activities." How dare we forget. She understands God's pictures. I was looking too hard to develop them in my own life. The development isn't in having the eyes to see; it's in having the body gathered to see. The identifying mark comes in community.

In the movie *Toy Story* Andy is a child who loves his toys. Buzz Lightyear and Woody, two of his favorites, end up, through a series of mishaps, in the home of his next-door neighbor. In no way does Andy's neighbor love his toys as Andy does. Lamenting their fate, Buzz and Woody feel pretty unworthy. When Buzz is feeling down, Woody offers a word of encouragement. So in turn, Buzz bolsters Woody's day with a reminder of whose he is. "Andy loves you," is all he needs to say. Even with those words, Buzz looks skeptically down at his arm. Feeling insignificant and unworthy, he says, "I'm just a stupid little insignificant toy," as he flips up a flap to reveal the mark "Made in Taiwan." But a little while later he looks down at his shoe and remembers what is written on his sole: "Andy," it simply says. Nothing wrong with Taiwan, but this other mark claims the life of Buzz. Through this signature he knows whose he is. Just when his wax begins to chip away, the picture is rolled out again for him through a signature on his sole.

We are marked with the name of Christ in baptism and in Communion. The sacraments sign this name upon our souls and seal it upon our hearts. Not only do they signify to us the claim of God on our lives and seals this upon our hearts, but also through the sacraments God *delivers* us from evil. We know what happens when the clay crumbles and the wax chips. The world can be a messy and broken place. There is something about a crumb of bread, a sip of wine and a sprinkling of water that reminds us that evil and brokenness, death and sorrow, will not have the last word.

The sacraments remind us that God delivered the people of Israel out of slavery, delivered them through the Red Sea, and delivered them to the promised land. The sacraments proclaim that Christ did not remain dead and buried, but he rose again and ascended into heaven. In Communion it becomes clear that despite betrayal and even death, God has the last word: "This is my body, broken for you, do this in remembrance of me." In baptism God speaks again with the gracious words "You are my Beloved, with whom I am well pleased."

Stevie Wonder didn't intend to sing about the sacraments. He was singing about love. But isn't that what the sacraments are all about? Maybe it is a love letter that goes something like this: "In the beginning, God created the world and populated it with children. They were cute and wonderful, but they made a mess. God added some animals, all sorts of them, but things got even messier. So God created men and women, and well, we still keep messing things up. So God created something we can hold onto, something tangible in the midst of a broken world to be a visible sign of God's invisible love and grace. God gave us a crumb of bread, a sip of bitter wine and the running water of baptism. . . ."

With this bread and wine, with just a few droplets of water, God says to us as loud as possible, "I am yours." I am for you even when it feels like the whole world is against you. And in our receiving of these gifts, we whisper the same thing back, "I'm yours, God. I'm yours."

Baptism

Water, stories, the body,
all the things we do, are mediums
that hide and show what's hidden.
Study them,
and enjoy this being washed
with a secret we sometimes know,
and then not.

          —Rumi, *"Water, stories, the body"*[1]

*T*oday I know the secret. It was whispered to me as the monsoon rains finally began to fall. For those who don't understand the desert, "monsoon" may seem a misnomer. One-hundredth of an inch of rain is hardly a monsoon and yet it marked the end of over one hundred days without a drop of rain. One-hundredth of an inch of water is all it takes to get the town talking. One-hundredth of an inch of water makes the ocotillo flower and the brittlebush brighten. One-hundredth of an inch of rain, believe it or not, can cause the dry riverbeds to run with water. One-hundredth of an inch of rain was overwhelming to the senses; tears surfaced and tensions eased. People around town were kinder; laughter bubbled and children danced in the droplets. My whole body had been aching for a storm. Everything within me needed that washed clean feeling to remove the dust and dirt that had accumulated over the past one hundred days. Now, finally, not only was I washed, but the secret was revealed. It doesn't take much to feel renewed and washed clean. I gulped it down.

Anyone who has ever lived in the desert or through a drought knows how precious and holy water is. Drops are never taken for granted. When those drops begin to fall you realize how long it's been; it takes a moment to remember how to turn on the windshield wipers. It wasn't until I moved to the desert that I saw my first store-front dedicated entirely to water. There are water drive-throughs to speedily fill up with a new supply. The provision of water by faith-based groups for migrants crossing the border is a controversial topic. The sound of a few drops of water poured from pitcher into basin calls to mind streams, rivers and oceans.

It is these drops that make their identifying mark on us as a body of Christ. These drops cling and claim that God is faithful, sin has been washed away and we have been reborn. The stories trickle down—creation, the flood, the exodus from Egypt. The water seals us in God's Spirit and wraps around us the fresh garment of Christ. We are washed and adopted into Christ's family, the church. The water pulses with life, new life in the resurrected Christ, who reigns over and rains down. It doesn't take much, just a few drops, to remind us of all this, one-hundredth of an inch sprinkling out from the waters of eternity.

A friend's parents recently visited the Dead Sea. Eager for their son to be ordained as a pastor, and perhaps even more eager for him to have a child one day so they could be grandparents, they brought him a bottle of water taken from the sea to be used either at his first baptism as a pastor or the baptism of their first grandchild. Touched by their gift, but in a rush, he put the bottle in his dorm room refrigerator. That night he and a friend returned from a heated basketball game. "Can I grab a drink of water from your fridge?" his friend asked. Gulping down the salty, gritty water of the Dead Sea was satisfying for only a second. Spitting it out his friend gasped, "What is this stuff?" Sometimes the water of baptism can be misappropriated. It becomes stagnant—something we want to swallow up for our own merit, or something we superstitiously go through as a right of passage. It becomes stagnant when the vows stay in the sanctuary instead of spilling out into the lives and the community of the church.

One desert church has a baptismal font that runs continually. No stagnant water here. The sound of its bubbling provides the backdrop for worship. Whether there is a baptism or not that day, there is the continual reminder of the faithfulness of God that is live-giving and always spilling over into our lives. During the confession, the water runs. In the quiet of a prayer, the water laps and purls. Gathering around the Word, proclaiming it, responding to the gospel, celebrating the sacraments and bearing all of this out into the world are counterpoints to the ongoing melody of gurgling grace. This is a church that takes seriously the call to have justice roll down like waters and righteousness like an ever-flowing stream. This congregation takes to heart Jesus' offering the gift of living water. Two years ago they partnered with another congregation to begin providing water in the desert along the paths frequently traversed by migrant workers. This congregation knows that God's redeeming grace is offered to all people.

It is that grace that adopts us into the covenant family of the church. Baptism is both corporate and individual. One of the most meaningful baptisms I participated in happened as a result of an adoption. Anna and Tom had tried for years to conceive. Certainly there is a story like theirs in your congregation. After years of failure, the adoption finally came through. When the phone call came, Anna and Tom were caught totally by surprise. "Your son has arrived. You may take him home tomorrow morning," the caller heralded. Without a moment to prepare and not one diaper in the house, they rushed out that evening to the distant location to spend the night and be ready to receive him first thing in the morning. They met their son and knew God's faithfulness. But it wasn't until they returned home the next day that they knew fully what it meant to be part of the body of Christ. A women's circle from the church had covertly broken into their home and set up a nursery. Furniture, baby outfits, diaper pail, and piles of Pampers welcomed them all home. Putting on the fresh garment of Christ? Why not one of those soft, cotton baby garments?

A few years later, Tom and Anna had the opportunity to adopt another child. Her mother made one request during the adoption, that the child would be baptized by immersion. It wasn't that the birth mother wanted her to choose her baptism; she simply wanted her baptism to be an overwhelming sign of Michelle's adoption into the covenant family of the body of Christ. It wasn't until fifteen years later that Michelle was baptized. We borrowed the immersion pool at the church across the street and invited the congregation to come. It takes only a few drops to declare the adoption, but when the pool of water is so big that the congregation could practically jump in as well, one just can't help but be not only reminded but convicted and claimed by the fact that we are all part of this family. "See what love God has for us that we should be called children of God, and so we are."

As a child, hearing those familiar words, "See what love God has for us . . . ," the claim was easy to accept as my own. Why does it get harder as we age? Last Sunday in worship the pastor ended the baptism with a whisper into the ear of the child that was just overheard by the gathered congregation: "Oh, you are a bundle of love. I don't want to put you down. But there comes a time when we have to let go and then trust that the Lord will uphold you forever."

We are upheld through the Lord, by the church. There is talk these days in our postmodern context of a shift from a solid culture to a liquid culture. A few theologians have understood this transformation for the church as well. If the church is going to be relevant today, then we need to be a liquid church.[2] While solids are bound together, holding their shape through the strength of the atoms, liquids are fluid. As Rodger Nishioka writes, "They travel easily. They flow, spill, run out, splash, pour, leak, flood, spray, drip, seep and ooze. They are not easily stopped. When being subjected to stress . . . liquids do not hold their shape."[3] Now, you might be thinking that we want the church to hold its shape, particularly if the culture is constantly in a state of changing fluidity. Nishioka goes on to explain, "The solid church is a one-size-fits-all church. Accommodate to us or go somewhere else." Anyone who has heard the dreaded seven last words of the church, "We haven't done it that way before," knows the frustrations of solidity. On the other hand, "the liquid church is fluid and agile and responds to stresses—even welcoming them, for this is the nature of living."

Life in a liquid church is as inviting as the cool pool of water in the baptismal basin; it is as challenging as the movement from death to resurrected life in the dunking; and it is as comforting as the blessing "See what love God has for us that we should be called children of God." As the baptized, we know the refreshment and the freedom and the movement found in water. It is this liquid blessing that flows out of our lives, spills into our days, runs out into the streets where we live, splashes our neighbor, pours out on strangers, leaks into conversation and floods the world with the grace of God. Spraying, dripping, seeping, oozing, the liquid blessing of baptism pours out into the lives claimed at baptism.

Taoism has long understood this concept of being water. Their doctrine upholds a principle called "wu wei." Wu wei is the principle of flexibility and adaptiveness to one's surroundings that creates openness and effectiveness. The image most often used to depict this concept is water. Water possesses the ability to nourish and adapt to its environment. Its suppleness and strength are unsurpassed. Its clarity comes through stillness. The *Tao Te Ching* notes,

> Nothing in the world
> is as soft and yielding as water.
> Yet for dissolving the hard and inflexible,
> nothing can surpass it.
>
> The soft overcomes the hard;
> the gentle overcomes the rigid.
> Everyone knows this is true,
> but few can put it into practice.[4]

As Christians, bathed in this water, our lives are about figuring out how to put that liquid blessing into practice. How do we practice being liquid? How are we soft and yielding? We practice baptism by recognizing that our actions and words are mediums that reveal what is at times hidden—God's grace. As the Directory for Worship of the Presbyterian Church asserts, "Baptism is God's gift of grace and also God's summons to respond to that grace."[5] Practicing baptism means accepting that grace and being that grace to others. Some days I don't know which is a harder call. To claim it and know it for myself or to pour out that grace on the strangers and loved ones around me. As Christians, it is not the water but our God who pours the drops and possesses this power. Christ was able to put it into practice and showed us the way of grace and truth and love. Now it is in our hands to try and respond to that grace poured out.

As a new mom, I spend a lot of time in a liquid world. Cups of milk, drinks of water, splashes of the bathtub are mopped up over and over again each day. Solids are a lot easier to be around than liquids. There is an old story of parents being a liquid blessing to their son. After cleaning and cooking and setting the table, parents and a young child sit down to the dinner table. Reaching for his first sip of milk, the son spills his milk across the table. What he expected, a bristled reprimand, was not what he received. His mom spilled her milk, and then again his dad. It's a story we tell again and again because we are all too familiar with the bristled reprimand. Even though we don't want to believe it's what we would expect, we know it is so. What demands its retelling is the spillage of unexpected grace. The soft overcomes the hard and the gentle overcomes the rigid. That grace takes root and grows.

Hildegaard of Bingen coined the word *viriditas* to describe the greening power of God that brings growth and fruitfulness to even the dryest of places.[6] The waters of baptism remind us that it doesn't take much for that greening power to take effect. It is a mysterious process, but readily evidenced. Many plants in the desert call for the question "Are you dead yet?" But one-hundredth of an inch of water draws out the green leaves of the ocotillo and gives a viable bend to the leaves of the otherwise brittle bush. Just when we as a community of faith, as individuals seeking to be faithful followers of Christ, ask the same question of ourselves, we overhear that secret whispered in the baptismal waters—it doesn't take much, just a few drops, for God's grace to be poured out upon us.

Several years ago, my father, a Presbyterian pastor, was leading a class on baptism for parents and their children. Having gone through the routine teaching from the *Book of Order* peppered by a few personal anecdotes, he asked at the end if there were any questions. Sam, a young boy of about seven, raised his hand. Whether the latest Harry Potter puzzling plot absorbed him or he simply had a heart for the intriguing, we'll never know. Who knows if he was looking for trap doors and hidden rooms or delving into the depths of theology. But his question was earnest and probing: "Does this church have any mysteries?" Yes, Sam, it does. Sometimes we know these mysteries and sometimes we do not. Study them, but in the meantime, enjoy being washed.

Communion

For the memories themselves are not important. Only when
they have changed into our very blood, into glance and ges-
ture, and are nameless, no longer to be distinguished from
ourselves—only then can it happen that in some very rare
hour the first word of a verse arises in their midst and goes
forth from them.

—*Rainer Maria Rilke,*
The Notebooks of Malte Laurids Brigge[1]

Do this in remembrance of me." The words etched into the Communion table are the clearest memory I have of worship as a young child. Amid all the sermons, music, children's sermons, sacraments and holidays, these words are what I remember most. I couldn't tell you the color of the walls or the carpet, the shape of the sanctuary, the tint of the windows, but the Communion table was white with a wooden top. Carved into the side, just underneath the wooden top, were these words. Being so young, the meaning in the phrase was less a theological injunction and much more an invitation to engage in the mystery present both in worship and in sacrament. The phrase is deceptively simple, easy enough for a young child to read and remember, complex enough to take a lifetime to unravel its meaning.

Over the course of my life, "Do this in remembrance of me" has taken on many layers of meaning. For many years it was simply about not forgetting. While each week brought many ways of failing to remember I was a child of God—on the playground, among my peers, pressures to fit into the crowd—Sunday mornings called me to remember something else. I was loved, I was forgiven and I was claimed. With all these blessings came a challenge to live differently. Some days I did; many days I didn't.

One Sunday morning I brought a Catholic boyfriend to church. We celebrated Communion that day, and the "little" cups surprised him. He was used to going forward for the common cup. After receiving the grape juice he began to giggle. My mom nudged, as did I, and his laughter ceased until after worship. Once the service was over he explained what tickled him. "I just kept remembering that scene in 'Raiders of the Lost Ark' with all those little shot glasses," he said.

What we are called to remember in Communion is, of course, much deeper than a movie scene. It is the screenplay of Christ's life, death and resurrection offered for us as the body of Christ. It is a story of forgiveness and sacrifice and promise. Forgetting any of these things negates the meaning of Communion, and yet remembering alone is not enough for full participation in the sacrament.

This was a principal struggle during the Reformation. The doctrine of transubstantiation became a fancy way of saying that the outward appearance of bread and wine did not change, but the substance present within them changed to the very person of Jesus Christ. The Roman Catholic Church offered a statement in 1551, "The Decree on the Most Holy Sacrament of the Eucharist," which clearly stated, "After the consecration of the bread and wine, our Lord Jesus Christ is truly, really and substantially contained in the venerable sacrament of the holy Eucharist under the appearance of those physical things." To counterpoint this claim, Martin Luther presented the idea of consubstantiation. There is no change in substance, he claimed. Instead, both the elements and Jesus Christ are fully present simultaneously. The body of Christ is "in, with, under, around and behind the bread and the wine."

It was Huldrych Zwingli who disputed both of these doctrinal claims. Zwingli eliminated the real presence of Christ at the Eucharist by saying the Lord's Supper is "a memorial to the suffering of Christ, and not a sacrifice." In other words, we are called to remember Christ's life instead of experiencing the real presence of Christ at the table. But for the Reformers, remembering was not enough. This meal is more than a memorial meal. Something happens in Communion that is, as Augustine would say, "a visible sign of the invisible love and grace of God." This visible sign calls us beyond memory to a new way of living. To focus on recollection is not enough; this recollection calls us to action, for we "*Do* this in remembrance. . . ."

Perhaps the greater question in our lives today is less about what the bread and the wine become, and much more a question of who *we* become as we partake of the bread and the wine. As my understanding of Communion grew, I moved beyond the concept of remembering as simply "not forgetting." Of course, this was an element of my celebration of Communion, but it was not the end. To remember became a very active process when I realized that in some sense remembering is the opposite of dis-membering. Our world is broken and so are we; even the body of Christ definitely knows fragmentation. To remember means doing something as we attend to the pieces that need putting back together. Though the nursery rhyme may have become ingrained at an early age—"Humpty Dumpty sat on a wall, Humpty Dumpty had a great fall, all the king's horses and all the king's men, couldn't put Humpty together again"—we know that Christ proves this rhyme false. There is the possibility of being put together through the sacrifice of Jesus Christ. Reconciliation and re-membering this broken body is a promise we hold on to.

A favorite story of mine has been on the Internet numerous times. Every once in a while I receive it again. A young boy greeted his father after work, eager to play. The father, tired after a long day, only wanted to put his feet up and read the paper. To buy himself a little time the dad took a section of the paper and ripped it into pieces as a puzzle for his son to put together. "Look, here's a picture of the world," he said, "see if you can put the pieces back together." Certain that the continents and oceans would keep his son adrift for a while as he figured out how to put them back together, the dad settled back into his easy chair to read the front page. In a matter of moments, the son returned. "Dad, I'm done!" Surprised the dad asked, "How did you finish so quickly?" The son responded, "It was easy, on the other side of the pieces was a picture of a person. To put the world back together, I put the pieces of the person back together first."

That's a story I could preach over and over again. But while I love the truth inherent in it, I know that re-membering a broken body takes more than putting the pieces of an individual back together. We are a broken community. Being active in putting this dismembered body back together means doing the reconciling work of healing. "Do this in remembrance of me," Christ commands his disciples in the upper room. This isn't an easy charge. It takes sacrifice and risk on our part to follow this injunction through to completion.

One of the most controversial Sundays in a church I once attended is Communion Sunday, celebrated once a month. Some members of the congregation actually worship in other churches on this day because of a point of disagreement they have regarding a section of the Communion liturgy. After the invitation is given, the statement is made, "The peace of the Lord be with you." The expected response is, "And also with you." After this litany, the pastor gives an invitation to turn to your neighbor with a word of peace. The folks who feel disgruntled about this piece of the liturgy argue that it is not only disruptive to worship, but it also feels "fake." While there is a degree of formality to the greeting, it is intended to be a symbolic action. We cannot come to the Communion table when we are not in harmony with our neighbor. While it might not be the person on our right or our left with whom we need reconciliation, our greeting them in peace is a reminder to leave worship and go make peace with those whom we have slighted or who have hurt us. The writer of Matthew's Gospel isn't speaking about Communion, but the intention is similar: "When you are offering your gift at the altar, if you remember that your brother or sister has something against you, leave your gift there before the altar and go; first be reconciled to your brother or sister, and then come and offer your gift" (Matt. 5:23–24). In other words, go do some active re-membering, go and pick up the pieces, be reconciled, and then come and "Do this in remembrance of me."

It's not just a question of what the bread and wine become, it is a question of who we become as we celebrate Communion. We become whole, we become one body, we become the body of Christ as we are reconciled to ourselves, to our neighbors and to our God. We become people who go courageously and humbly to pick up the pieces, to put the world back together again. "All the king's horses and all the king's men" couldn't solve poor Humpty Dumpty's problem, but we have the strength of a King who can, Christ our Lord who sits on the right hand of God. "Do this in remembrance of me" is a phrase that prompts our association with Jesus Christ as peacemaker and as king.

Recently, a Minute for Mission I heard in worship drew me toward an even deeper understanding of Communion. A woman had been undergoing chemotherapy for months, and in the midst of the process she became very ill and needed a blood transfusion. The church, eager to respond, hosted a blood drive for her. As she tried to express her deepest thanks to the congregation, she stumbled through the tears: "I have a whole new understanding of what it means to be the body of Christ. Your blood is my blood and my blood is made new by your blood. The blood of this congregation is pumping through my veins and I would not be standing here to tell you if it weren't for this body of Christ." Her Communion with this body of Christ had been internalized in such a deep way that now it was her very own pulse and flow of life.

In his only full-scale novel, *The Notebooks of Malte Laurids Brigge*, Rainer Maria Rilke develops the character of Malte, a young poet. Rilke challenges the theory that dismisses art and poetry as mere feeling. Instead, a poet experiences a progression of feelings and thoughts that lead to a deep, internal, life-changing kind of knowing. Artistic expression grows from feeling through experiences through memories through forgetting to what can be called "blood-remembering." From this blood-remembering poetry is born. As Rilke writes,

> For the memories themselves are not important. Only when they have changed into our very blood, into glance and gesture, and are nameless, no longer to be distinguished from ourselves—only then can it happen that in some very rare hour the first word of a verse arises in their midst and goes forth from them.

The woman in the Minute for Mission knew in a deep way what blood-remembering was all about. She had internalized the depth of the gift from her congregation; their blood had turned to her blood; they had become glance and gesture. This could not be distinguished from her own self because now she was a part of a bigger body. This was not just something she remembered—it was much more than memory. It was not something she pieced together, as in a mental exercise of calling to mind. This wasn't a "heart" knowing or a "head" knowing; it wasn't based solely on feeling or reason. This was a full-bodied knowing, something she would never forget. She had deeply internalized the significance of the body and blood of Jesus Christ; these were present within her through the sacrifice of her church. The paradox was that while she had changed at the deepest of all possible levels, she was now more truly herself than ever.

Rilke writes that the result of this blood-remembering is that "the first word of verse arises in their midst and goes forth from them." While he is speaking of a poet's first word, we know as a Christian community what that first word really is. "In the beginning was the Word," begins the Gospel of John, "and the Word was with God, and the Word was God." The first word of our verse as a body of Christ has already been spoken; it is Christ himself. With that word comes a sacrifice, a promise and an invitation: "Do this in remembrance of me."

We don't just "take" Communion; we don't simply "remember" Communion. Communion is not something we just "do." "Do this in remembrance of me" calls us to full association with Christ as Lord and King; it forces us to full recollection of all God's people, and it prompts that the Holy Spirit direct our actions. We live, breathe and pulse Communion as we live out what it means to be the body of Christ. There is a full-bodied knowing to this phrase, "Do this in remembrance of me." It is a knowing that comes through "blood-remembering." Knowing internalized in this fashion is a knowing that pulses new life into the world.

Bearing Out

Bearing Out

History says, Don't hope
On this side of the grave.
But then, once in a lifetime
The longed-for tidal wave
Of justice can rise up,
And hope and history rhyme.

So hope for a great sea-change
On the far side of revenge.
Believe that a further shore
Is reachable from here.
Believe in miracles
And cures and healing wells.

Call miracle self-healing:
The utter, self-revealing
Double-take of feeling.
If there's fire on the mountain
Or lightning and storm
And a god speaks from the sky
That means someone is hearing
The outcry and the birth-cry
Of new life at its term.

Seamus Heaney, The Cure at Troy[1]

*T*he language of "bearing out" is unique to the Presbyterian tradition. Other denominations use the language of being "sent out" to describe the movement from worship into the world. Either means equipping the gathered to go out and live the gospel, but I prefer the wording "bearing out" for several reasons. The Directory for Worship states that the fifth movement of worship is "Bearing and Following the Word out into the World." What I love about these words is that we don't bear it out alone. We follow the Word, which has preceded us, out into the world. Christ has gone before us to prepare the way.

In Mark's Gospel a young man dressed in dazzling white encouraged the distraught visitors to the tomb: "He is going ahead of you to Galilee; there you will see him, just as he told you." This stranger is telling them to go against history and to hope on this side of the grave. Each Sunday as we receive the charge to go out into the world, we are encouraged to do the same—to hope for, as Seamus Heaney would offer, a great "sea-change" so that hope and history might rhyme. This work demands that we follow Christ into the world and bear the gospel out as best we can.

There are certainly times when we need encouragement to do this. Putting one foot in front of the other to go face the world isn't always easy. We go home to places of pain and loss. Life at times can feel completely unbearable. Ann Packer begins her novel *The Dive from Clausen's Pier* with these words:

> When something terrible happens to someone else, people often use the word "unbearable." Living through a child's death, a spouse's, enduring some other kind of permanent loss—it's unbearable, it's too awful to be borne, and the person or people to whom it's happened take on a kind of horrible glow in your mind, because they are in fact bearing it, or trying to: doing the thing that it's impossible to do.[2]

There are times when bearing out feels impossible. The hope expressed by the stranger in the tomb falls on deaf ears. Going to worship is an act of pure will, the ultimate expression of faith given the circumstances of life. But then to have to leave the safety of the sanctuary to go into the streets and face the unbearable parts of life seems impossible.

In Sophocles' play *Philoctetes,* the title character is in an unbearable situation. He has been abandoned by his comrades and marooned on a desert island because of a foul wound on his foot. Concerned for their own health, his shipmates abandon him. Years later, several reappear because they need a bow that only Philoctetes possesses. This is the bow that will win the Greeks the Trojan War. They need it and they need him for their victory. The irony of the story is that the lonesome island has become a sanctuary of sorts for him. Leaving is an act of faith. For Philoctetes, healing comes not only through surviving the unbearable time alone on the island but also through gathering the courage to leave and bear out a new life. To do so, he must relinquish anger so he can bear out a new life for himself and the world.

Bearing out carries with it a paradox. Sometimes we need to leave worship empty-handed, bearing out open arms instead of the clutched fists we bring in. Bearing out means leaving some things behind. Michael Lindvall says it well. Instead of asking, "What did you get out of that service?" he writes, "The better question might be: What did you lose in that service? What burden did you drop at the foot of the cross? What pride did you shed? What gnawing anger are you going home without? What lie do you no longer believe?"[3] Sometimes our bearing out into the world means leaving worship empty-handed and trusting that our hands are open to receive Christ on the road ahead.

But we also carry out something new into the world—while we leave some things behind, we also bear out a new vision, a new challenge to live up to the demands of the gospel. Our bearing out is a charge to make "hope and history rhyme." It means finding a way to make the unbearable rhyme with the bearable. In a dissonant world, making rhymes is a jarring task. Christ may be on the road ahead, but we are called to compose a few poems as we walk forward to meet him. What rhymes with war? What rhymes with fear? What rhymes with loneliness and loss? What rhymes with injustice, intolerance and insurmountable? Some words seem impossible to rhyme. Their syllabic makeup aside, it is their inherent nature that offers only discord. And we are called to make these histories rhyme with hope?

In a sermon on the love of Christ preached by Eugenia Gamble, she didn't offer rhymes, but she did offer a poem. She ended the sermon by saying, "I didn't know what to tell you all here about the love of God, and then it finally dawned on me that the love of God cannot be described or even approached. It sneaks up to us, it's caught like a wave from the corner of the eye and can only be communicated in tears. So I wrote you a poem." The poem she went on to preach was this:

> God's lightning love is like an ocean, emerald green,
> Cool and gentle in which we can see to the bottom and wiggle
>   our toes.
> It is like an ocean dark and churning all foam and unexpected
>   tumbles.
> It is like an oxygen mist with just a hint of albuterol that slips
>   new
> Life into scarred lungs and sets them free.
> It is like new glasses and spring flowers and poems by old
>   professors
> And sleeping dogs.
> It is like a drip of honey on a finger or like a mother lifting a car
> To free a child.
> It is like rain on parched clay,
> Like the little word "maybe" in the midst of despair.
> Like a photograph of old days that never end and like something
> Shiny, new and unbroken.
> It is like a hand offered for nails.
> It is like nothing we know and everything we long for.[4]

Even if we can't make rhymes, we can make tidal waves of poems to flood the world with something beyond the prose we know.

We are called to bear the Word out into the world in poetic fashion. It is a heavy task. Because it is heavy, there is wrapped up in the word "bearing" a sense of endurance. We bear with the incomplete. We bear with the fact that God's kingdom is not here yet. We bear with the knowledge that we live in the already/not-yet paradox of Christ's coming. We bear with the week and wait to be girded up again on Sunday to go out and do it again. The way we endure is with hope. Augustine wrote, "Hope has two daughters, anger and courage." Anger, he meant, at the injustice and incompleteness of the world. We must have courage to go and make change. The great sea change, the changes we hope to see, come through the perseverance to face the world with anger and with courage.

On 34th Street in New York City, the New York Public Library is a pillar of possibilities. The front steps lead into stacks of hopes and dreams. On either side of the steps are two stone lions. Sitting there on the steps one day, I wondered about these graceful creatures on either side of me. Wandering over I read the name of the first, Patience, and the second, Fortitude. I realized in that moment I had been sitting between Patience and Fortitude. It was a divine word at that moment in my life as I faced questions about the future. So we sit between patience and fortitude in the life of faith. Patiently we wait for God's unveiling. We believe in miracles and cures and healing wells, but they do not always happen in our good timing. Patiently we wait for that longed-for tidal wave, but it doesn't always tumble over into the world as planned. Yet we do not just wait around; we continue to build up, to write poems, to fight injustice, to fortify.

The work of fortifying is not glamorous; it is the hard work of details, sweat, persistence and vision. There's an old story of three guys laying bricks. When asked why they are doing it, the first says, "I'm doing it for the wages." The second replies, "I'm doing it for my family." The third says, "I'm helping to build a cathedral." Our fortifying, our bearing out, is about building up that cathedral in the world so the sanctuary itself is not the only sanctuary. God has a vision bigger than the walls of our churches, a vision that means laying bricks throughout the world. It's hard work, often unnoticed and unappreciated, but a beautiful cathedral will be the result.

At Princeton University a few years ago, Johnathan Kozol addressed a group of college students. His talk poured out from his experiences in the South Bronx working as a teacher and writing about his days as a journalist. His time there is recorded in his book *Amazing Grace*. That night he preached as he told the students about his year of "miracles and ashes." He described the ashes of incinerators placed in that community creating so much dust that the majority of children had asthma and carried inhalers. He talked about ashes of lives lost to drugs and gang warfare. He talked about ashes of dreams and hopes. But there were miracles there as well. He told of Margaret, a Yale-educated lawyer who sacrificed everything to come into the community and run an after-school center.

As he finished describing his year of miracles and ashes, he opened the conversation to the audience for questions. "What should we do?" asked the first person to raise a hand. Kozol replied, "I knew that would be the first question and that question makes me mad. You don't need to ask me what to do. You know what needs to be done. The question really is do you have the courage to go out and actually do it?" You don't need me to describe the silence in that auditorium. Everyone knew he was right. Pastors charging us with the command to "bear and follow the Word into the world" are usually a bit more restrained in their challenge.

We are that longed-for tidal wave that can bear justice into the world. Do we have the anger and the courage, do we have the patience and the fortitude, to make hope and history rhyme?

Closing Hymn

He sings in his father's arms, sings his father
to sleep, all the while seeing how on that face
grown suddenly strange, wasting to shadow,
time moves. Stern time. Sweet time. Because his father

asked, he sings; because they are wholly lost.
How else, in immaculate noon, will each find
each, who are so close now? So close and lost.
His voice stands at windows, runs everywhere.

You must sing to be found; when found you must sing.
                              —*Li-Young Lee, "You Must Sing"*[1]

*I*n certain African tribes, before a child is born into this world, a group
of elders from the community remove themselves from the noise of
the tribe to deeply listen for the song of the unborn child. Once their
collective ears have heard the song of this child, they return from the
wilderness to the birthing. There they sing the child into the world.
From then on at key points in the life of the growing child the community sings the specially written song to him or her. On the first day
of school, on entering adulthood, on joining together in marriage their
unique song is sung. The song is sung upon special occasions, but there
is one other occasion that might bring out the drums as well. If there
is ever a time in childhood or in adult life that the individual com-
mits a crime or an aberrant social act, their song is sung to them by
their community. Outrage and disappointment are unleashed through

singing. Justice is achieved by song. Remembrance of created identity is claimed in song. The lost are found in singing.

Our spiritual soundtrack in the church begins at baptism. It is at the basin of water we find our created identity; we claim it in the sacrament and in song. At a small church of just twenty or so members in California, the congregation gathers around the baptismal font and sings to the baptized these words in the tune of "Morning Has Broken":

> (Name of child), we name you: And with thanksgiving,
> Offer our prayer and sing you this song.
> We are the church, your spiritual family.
> Sing we our praises to Christ the Lord.
>
> Children we all are, of God the creator;
> Risking and loving, daring to see
> The heavenly kingdom growing among us.
> Sing we our praises to Christ the Lord.[2]

I hope at no matter what age of the child's life, she or he will remember that tune and in remembering it, find once again the promise made at baptism.

Several summers ago I had the opportunity to officiate the wedding of a couple who had both been divorced. After years of heartbreak, they had found love once again in each other. For both, music was foundational in their lives. The woman spoke of singing as a place of finding peace and a center. The man shared memories of singing with his daughters—happy times around the piano singing the songs of their faith. Both spoke of deep gratitude for their friends who had grounded them both through the hard times. Repeating the old saying, one of them said, "A friend is someone who knows your song and sings it back to you when you have forgotten it." Wanting to thank their friends for their faithfulness through this difficult time of life, they wrote new verses to the old "Resignation" tune to be sung as a prayer at their wedding. These words expressed both what they had lost, and what they had found:

> All beautiful this wedding day with blessings from above,
> The hand that shaped the rose has brought the beauty of
>   this love,

Unfolding from the thorns of life, new flowers delight this place,
The changing seasons of our lives are steadied by God's grace.

The friends and family gathered round have been God's
    helping hand,
Once tears and sadness flowed within, now joy and love abound,
God's sure provisions manifest in love encircled here,
From hand to hand, and heart to heart, God's providence
    made clear.

The church sings on. Through childhood and confirmation, through weddings and graduations, through baptism and Communion, through struggles and celebrations, through adulthood and funerals. As life circles and winds, working its way through the messy circumstances and tough decisions we make, these songs gain meaning. One youth group whom I worked with had the voices of angels. The congregation looked forward to their sharing of hymns and anthems in worship and on Christmas Eve in particular. One of the beloved songs was "Siyahamba," an African phrase meaning "We are moving in the light of God." The words were as simple as these, sung over and over again. The song concluded beyond words, with a deep humming of the memorable tune. As we shared years together in youth ministry, the song gained layers. One summer it was sung in an airport. The din of ticketing, luggage and crowds softened to hear the music. The terminal was quiet even after the humming had ended. College students returning at Christmas were welcomed home with song. A mission trip to Puerto Rico added verses in Spanish. A late night moose-hunting expedition on a mission trip to Maine added the silly "We are moosing in the light of God." The song was sung over and over again, each time adding a layer of memory to it. The song was sung so many times some lovingly called it "the youth group cheer." Years after I left the church, a former member of the youth group, Andrew, died of cancer. He was just 23. Reading through the funeral service my heart stopped when I read the postlude anthem. "Siyahamba," it said. Andrew was moving in the light of God.

The music of the church finds layers of meaning as hymns are sung year after year. We find in their words ourselves—sometimes lost, sometimes found. We find in their tunes the depth and mystery of

God's creative anthem being directed from above. There is no better song about the lost being found than "Amazing Grace." "Amazing grace, how sweet the sound, that saved a wretch like me! I once was lost but now am found, was blind but now I see." There is something about worship and music and song that guide us through the mazes of life and into a whole new realm of foundation for how we live. We are found standing dumbfounded amidst the tangled mazes of our lives. There we lose the determination we had to lose God and discover that God had found us out all along.

Sometimes when I am singing in worship, I worry about being found solely by my out-of-tune voice. At times I find that I have sung through half of a song and have no idea what the words are truly saying. I attempt to keep singing while at the same time backtracking through the words to discover their meaning. Then there are the times when I find myself at a much deeper place. It is in that place I find the things I have lost. Singing, "Take my life and let it be, consecrated, Lord, to thee," I find that I have forgotten this week how my life is not my own. Singing, "My Shepherd will supply my need; Jehovah is his name: In pastures fresh he makes me feed, beside the living stream. He brings my wandering spirit back, when I forsake his ways, and leads me, for His mercy's sake, in paths of truth and grace," I find my wandering spirit being drawn back in. Singing, "The church's one foundation is Jesus Christ her Lord," I find that the church forgets what it is all about sometimes. Through the music of worship, we add songs to the soundtracks of our lives. While we might not have one song revealed for us through the tribal community, we do have a spiritual soundtrack that helps us find our way home.

Some mornings I wake up to my husband, Jason, singing in the shower. He starts with "Though I may speak with bravest fire, and have the gift to all inspire, but have not love. . . ." This is his getting-into-tune song. Crackling at first, sputtering with the start of the shower, his voice gets warmed up to the tune of "O Waly Waly." By "Take My Life" he has found his pitch. Verses pour out as written originally by Frances Ridley Havergal in 1874, and then he will make up a few of his own. Each morning brings a new verse, a prayer sung for the day. By the time he begins "Siyahamba," he is usually turning off the shower. "We are moving in the light of God, we are moving in the light of God . . ." becomes his song for ironing and getting dressed. The power of these songs is found in the memories they bring. Memories of our wedding day, June 26, 1999: through his daily singing of the music sung at our wedding, he remembers what our life together is all about. He finds again his love for me and his commitment to our life together. He sings to be found some days. Other days, knowing with joy what we have found in our life together, the only response is to sing.

Week after week the church sings the hymns of our faith. We sing to remember, we sing to be found, we sing with joy because we have been found, we sing to forget ourselves and to find again our center in God. From baptism on, our lives find meaning in these songs of faith. We sing each week wrapped in the arms of our father God, our mother God, singing with joy and thanksgiving, singing with lament and tears. In the stern times of our lives, in the sweet times, we sing. When we are wholly lost, we sing to be found. When we are wholly found, we sing to be lost in the love of our Lord Jesus Christ.

Benediction

Since there is no place large enough
to contain so much happiness,
you shrug, you raise your hands, and it flows out of you
into everything you touch. You are not responsible.
You take no credit, as the night sky takes no credit
for the moon, but continues to hold it, and share it,
and in that way, be known.
          —Naomi Shihab Nye, *"So Much Happiness"*[1]

*W*hen I was little, I used to raise my hand to receive the benediction. My mom, thinking I was mocking the pastor, who happened to be my dad, asked me not to do it. No part of me was mocking the pastor, but I had no recourse with my mom. I didn't have the words at that age to describe the need I felt to raise my hand and for that benediction to flow into me. It wasn't enough to stand still to receive the benediction; worship felt large enough, containing so much happiness, I needed to receive it in a tangible way. I have never seen anyone else raise a hand for the benediction until I met my husband. Though I have gotten shy and reserved, he still raises his hand Sunday after Sunday to internalize the blessing received in the benediction.

In the benediction, two prayers are lifted as the pastor's hands are raised. The first prayer is an injunction—a charge—to go, do, act, make happen. "Go out into the world in peace, have courage, hold onto what is good, return no one evil for evil, strengthen the fainthearted; support the weak, and help the suffering; honor all people; love and serve the Lord, rejoicing in the power of the Holy Spirit." Besides the words uttered after a baptism, these are the words that made the biggest impact on my childhood. The possibility of doing these things was in my hands. I gained hope and courage in hearing these words. The second prayer is an invocation—a blessing, a blessing to be held, a blessing to simply be, a blessing to dwell in the grace of the Lord Jesus Christ, the love of God and the communion of the Holy Spirit.

The word "benediction" at its roots means to "speak well of." There is also a sense in the benediction that in its asking God's blessing on someone, it almost speaks wellness into being. The great priestly benediction, "May the Lord bless you and keep you, may the Lord's face shine upon you and be gracious to you this day and always," is more than speaking nice things about someone. It is an injunction to invoke that wellness into being through the spoken word.

Cider House Rules is a complex movie about abortion and adoption. Michael Caine oversees an orphanage, loving the children into their adulthood. He is also a doctor who is willing when necessary to perform an abortion. The gray between these two callings is made even hazier through the inhalation of laughing gas he takes to ease his own pains. He is a broken man, but he is also an embodiment of grace. The scene that stands out for me in the complexity of the movie is simple. It is a bedtime story and tucking in the twenty or so boys in the orphanage. The evening is a steadying ritual, a chapter of a story, one that leaves you waiting for the next time with eager anticipation, and a benediction of sorts as he flips off the light switch. "Good night you princes of Maine, you kings of New England." As the light dims, one of the boys asks another, "Why does he do that?" "I don't know," his friend replied. "Do you like it when he does that?" he continues. "Yeah. I do."

It's a benediction because it is a blessing. It speaks well of these boys who are constantly holding out their hands to receive a handout, a hand-me-down, a handshake of potential adopted parents. Nothing is handed over easily to these kids, except for these words of blessing. The words speak well of them and at the same time call into possibility a greater reality, a bigger hope, a royal claim on their lives. Are they princes? No. Are they kings? No. Will they ever be? No. But is life in a royal kingdom a possibility for them? Absolutely.

Michael Caine is not a happy man in the movie. He and Pollyanna would not have much to talk about. But there is something bigger than him present in his words, and that something is too large to be contained within himself. It spills over. It is almost with a shrug of his shoulders that the blessing flows out of him into everything he touches. He makes known a royal kingdom that has been prepared for these orphan kids.

When I watched this movie I was struck at a deep level by the power of a blessing. Who was it, I wondered, who first experienced that overflow of happiness so much so that they had to make it known in the spoken word? Who uttered the first word of blessing? Did that person realize the power that a blessing holds to speak wellness into being even when everything about the given situation looked bleak?

Of course, it was God who generated the first blessings recorded in Genesis. God's blessing precedes any command or expectation of us. From the origin of creation we have been blessed. "So God created humankind in his image, in the image of God he created them; male and female he created them. God blessed them" (Gen. 1:27–28). Recently I heard a prayer, powerful in its overall truth, that began with these words: "Creator God, you have made us in your image. From the dust of the earth you have formed us and breathed our life into being. You bless us and you call us good. Since then, we have set about trying to prove you wrong." The prayer was honest in its recognition of our inability to pass on the blessing that we have been given. Why is it so hard to make it known? Is it that we don't recognize the blessings we have been handed, or is it that we want to clench them all for ourselves?

The first biblical figures to loosen their grasp and hand over a blessing to another beyond God were Rebekah's brothers before her marriage to Isaac. With collective voice they offered, "May you, our sister, become thousands of myriads; may your offspring gain possession of the gates of their foes" (Gen. 24:60). The blessing was offered in hopes of the great offspring promised to Abraham. Though God had promised Abraham as many ancestors as stars in the night sky, at this point in time the night sky still looked pretty dull. Yet Rebekah's brothers offer a reflection, like the moon, of God's promised blessing. They utter it again, hoping to speak wellness into being by praying for generations, myriads, stars to be born.

The college I attended was nestled into the Shenandoah Valley. On nights we needed a break from studying, we would drive up into the mountains to look up at the stars. There our world was enlarged from dorm life and textbook pages to a view filled with a myriad of possibilities. Their sparkling presence was a blessing. Later I learned that the word "Shenandoah" means "daughter of the stars." I took that name on as my own, letting myself be draped in that royal canopy. The phrase became a priestly benediction that offered both a charge and a blessing. The blessing was to remember the place from which I came, a place rich in possibility and promise. The charge was the responsibility that came with that promise. While life at times can feel limited by certain circumstances, God challenges us to live into a hope that is larger than any limitations. That hope is as wide as the sky and as sparkling as those stars.

Ultimately, blessing comes from God alone. But we are gifted with the capability to remind others of that promised blessing. Our words are charged with the power of God that enable us to see a landscape broader than our own view. We share the happiness we have received and pass it on so others might know the blessing. We hold it for a time, share it with a smile and make it known so that a royal kingdom might be realized.

Amen

Let it be . . .

—The Beatles

*W*anting to brush up on the classics, a friend recently purchased a used copy of *The Grapes of Wrath* to read on vacation. There on the beach, Sue journeyed through the Depression across Oklahoma and the plains into California. Feeling every pain and misfortune of the Joad family, she ached for them as the story drew her further and further in. As Sue neared the end of the book, she realized to her dismay that the last few pages were missing. Upon reading the last page left in her book, she was upset not just by the family's tragic story but by the fact she would have to wait to discover their fate.

It wasn't until Sue reached her hometown that she was able to run into the closest store to read the end of the story. There amid all the customers and aisles of books, she plopped on the floor of the literature section to read the final pages. Anyone who has ever read *The Grapes of Wrath* knows why she wept uncontrollably, among strangers and shoppers, as she turned to the very last page.

The appreciation for the ending grows in the living out of the story. For my friend, living with the uncertainty of the ending was hard, but then discovering the powerful image of God's provision found at the end was almost harder. Waiting is hard, but knowledge of grace and truth can be even harder. The ending has to do with the provision of nourishment when death seems to be the only viable option.

I love Sue's story, because if I had been reading the book, I would have read the last pages first. I never would have made it all the way home and into the bookstore with any sense of peace. There is no way I could have let it be. I would have called a friend, surfed the net, begged the local librarian to tell me the ending. It is a terrible habit I have, and as much as I might say, "Live into the ending," I have a hard time doing that myself. I want certainty, control, answers and a knowledge of what is to come. I can't live with the questions. I recently confessed this character flaw to my book group, asking for an assurance of pardon and permission to continue in the group. Thankfully, it was granted.

It is a blessed thing that as much as life feels tenuous and uncertain at times, God's end of the story for us is a very clear and certain "Amen." "Let it be," God assures us, for God alone knows where the story is going. God's answers for our lives and for our world are not expressed like the whim of a Magic Eight Ball, where we shake and shake and then wait for the answer to appear in the murky window. "Answer unclear," it might say, or "Try again later," or upon rare occasion, "It is decidedly so."

God's answer is always a "decidedly so." It's an "Amen" over and over again. A hearty amen, so be it, for us and for our world. "Amen" is a word that throughout Scripture expresses God's fixed and constant nature. With every "Amen" we utter in worship, we are turning the page, closing that chapter in our lives as we let it be into God's future. With that "Amen," we are affirming God's fixed and constant nature that gives us a good glimpse into the last pages of the story. The Hebrew word *amen* affirms certainty and faithfulness, and it is with these qualities that we live into the future. Throughout Scripture, from the "All the people shall say 'Amen'" of Deuteronomy to the "Amen and Amen" of the Psalms to the final word in Revelation, Scripture tells us, "Let it be" with certainty, "Let it be" with trustfulness, "Let it be" with faithfulness, for God knows the end of the story.

In worship, we tell the story of God over and over again each week. What is amazing about this word "Amen" is that all of the biblical story is encapsulated into this one final word. In worship we affirm that. We live out the story through our gathering, proclaiming, responding, sealing and bearing out. The chapters are fixed, the narrative is certain, but the details emerge anew every week. All of the narrative in between testifies to the salvation story. As Tom Long writes, "To go through the order of worship is symbolically to walk through the whole narrative of faith. The service is a metaphor constantly pointing to its referent."[1] The challenge for us is to continue that story as we walk out of the doors and into our lives so that the chapters of worship read the same as the pages of our lives.

To walk out of worship changed, worship must express where we are, our real feelings and real struggles, and prepare us for the challenges of fighting injustice and oppression. If we move through the story of salvation in our worship so that it comes alive for us, then we too will be able to say a hearty amen.

In his book *Let Everybody Say Amen*, Nigel Robb deepens the definition in this way: "[Amen] expresses submission and acceptance of the will of God. To say 'Amen' is to commit ourselves as individual members of the community of faith to what has been said. The utterance proclaims that we are putting ourselves at God's disposal."[2] Worship needs to move us to that place of commitment, but so does the worshiping life, the day-to-day living and bearing this out, so that each morning and each evening we can assuredly say "Amen" to the day, "Amen" to how God has used us.

While this all sounds great in the pages of a book, we all know that living worship can be a challenge. The future hovers uncertainly, questions gnaw, doubts cause worry. Headed to a church meeting one evening, I was uncertain about the outcome of an important vote. Even more so, I was concerned for our new senior pastor, who was still settling into a new call. Unable to postpone the discussion any longer, the session faced a divisive topic and one that would define the pastor's tenure in this new congregation. As I walked to the meeting early to gather my thoughts, I heard the peaceful sound of a piano being played nearby: "Let it be . . . Let it be. . . ." I recognized the familiar tune of the Beatles' classic and began to hum along. Then I realized it was a prayer. Sure enough, behind the piano sat the new pastor prayerfully playing the chords into the future with a resonant "Amen."

It is hard to live into the uncertainty, for we are people who want to skip to the last page. But the last page says this: With certainty. So be it. Let it be. Amen. The momentum and magnitude of the biblical story end with this affirmation. So does our worship, and so does the worshiping life. Amen.

Postlude

"Fireflies"

The Lord said:
Because these people draw near me
with their mouths and honor me with their lips,
while their hearts are far from me,
and their worship of me is a human commandment
learned by rote;
so I will again do amazing things with this people,
shocking and amazing.
                                        —Isaiah 29:13–14b

In the summer haze of dusk
our slow-bodied children laze their path
through wind-bent grass,
jars in hand, reaping a harvest of light.

We sit in dusk's respite, friends
gathering round to share the day's end, young
abandon reminding us to let today's worries
be enough for today, learning anew
the words and silences of truth, casting off
the hardening of heart learned by rote.
We are learning;
watch for the light instead
of settling down in the dark.

Our children teach us;
reach when it comes, anticipate
its crawl over our bodies, our limbs, tangle it
in our hair, hold it in open hands. We listen
as shouts of joy, dismay, trying again,
float over the fields, songs of giggles
and laughter shocked forth by living light
flashing for eyes to see.

Bits of light,
too fragile
to hold or keep. We anticipate,
amazing things, we hold
fast with friends and family,
waiting for the time when we all
will blaze and be taken home
in a harvest song of grace.

—Jason Hickman

Notes

GATHERING

1. Rainer Maria Rilke, *Rilke: Poems*, translated by J. B. Leishman (New York: Alfred A. Knopf, 1996), p. 151.

CALL TO WORSHIP

1. Mary Oliver, *Dream Work* (New York: Atlantic Monthly Press, 1986), p. 14.
2. David Brooks, *Bobos in Paradise: The New Upper Class and How They Got There* (New York: Simon and Schuster, 2001), pp. 218–19.

PRAYER OF INVOCATION

1. Thanks to Elizabeth Clark Thasiah for writing "Upon Adventure" for this chapter.
2. Annie Dillard, *Teaching a Stone to Talk* (New York: HarperCollins, 1982), p. 52.

OPENING HYMN

1. Rabindranath Tagore, *Gitanjali* (New York: Scribner Poetry, 1997), p. 29.
2. Josh Tyrangiel, "Bono," *Time* (March 4, 2002). Archived online at www.time.com.
3. Peter Gomes, *Sermons: Biblical Wisdom for Daily Living* (New York: Avon, 1998), p. 15.

CONFESSION

1. Anne Tyler, *Back When We Were Grownups* (New York: Ballantine, 2001), p. 3.

ASSURANCE OF PARDON

1. Paul Tillich, *Shaking of the Foundations* (New York: Charles Scribner's Sons, 1948), p. 162.

PROCLAIMING

1. Walt Whitman, "Song of Myself," in *Leaves of Grass* (New York: Barnes and Noble, 1993), p. 76.

2. Jane Golden, Robin Rice and Monica Yant Kinney, *Philadelphia Murals and the Stories They Tell* (Philadelphia: Temple University Press, 2002), p. 51.

3. Sharon Daloz Parks, "Faithful Becoming in a Complex World: New Powers, Perils and Possibilities," in *Growing Up Postmodern: Imitating Christ in the Age of 'Whatever,'* Institute for Youth Ministry, Princeton Theological Seminary (Princeton: Princeton Theological Seminary Office of Communications/Publications, 1998), pp. 46–47.

4. "Invisible to the Eye: A Commencement Address by Fred Rogers at the 1994 Pittsburgh Theological Seminary Graduation Exercises," in *Panorama: Pittsburgh Theological Seminary Bulletin* 43, no. 1 (2003): 7.

5. Jane Kenyon, "Briefly It Enters, and Briefly Speaks," in *Otherwise* (St. Paul: Graywolf Press, 1996), p. 115.

PRAYER FOR ILLUMINATION

1. Jane Kenyon, "Things," in *Otherwise* (St. Paul: Graywolf Press, 1996), p. 116.

CHILDREN'S SERMON

1. Carol Fleisher Feldman, quoted in Malcolm Gladwell, *The Tipping Point: How Little Things Can Make a Big Difference* (Waltham, MA: Little, Brown, 2002), p. 119.

2. Tom Junod, "Can You Say . . . Hero?" in *The Best Spiritual Writing*, ed. Philip Zaleski (San Francisco: HarperSanFrancisco, 1999), p. 149.

3. Johnathan Kozol, *Amazing Grace* (New York: Crown, 1995), pp. 237–39.

OLD TESTAMENT LESSON

1. John and Katherine Paterson, *Images of God* (Wilmington, MA: Clarion Books, 1998), p. 36.

NEW TESTAMENT LESSON

1. Wallace Stevens, "The Well Dressed Man With a Beard" in *Collected Poetry and Prose* (New York: Literary Classics of the United States, Inc., 1997), p. 224.

SERMON

1. David Whyte, "Loaves and Fishes," in *The House of Belonging* (Langley, WA: Many Rivers Press, 1997), p. 88.

2. Dean W. Chapman, *How to Worship as a Presbyterian* (Louisville: Geneva, 2001), pp. 69–73.

3. Barbara Brown Taylor, *When God is Silent* (Boston: Cowley, 1998), p. 51.

4. James E. Loder, *The Transforming Moment* (Colorado Springs: Helmers and Howard, 1989), pp. 3–4.

RESPONDING

1. Anne Morrow Lindbergh, *Gift from the Sea* (New York: Vintage, 1978), p. 23.

2. Frederick Buechner, *Wishful Thinking* (New York: Harper and Row, 1971), p. 95.

3. In most instances I use the NRSV for biblical references. Here I offer a modified translation.

4. Rebecca Wells, *The Divine Secrets of the Ya-Ya Sisterhood* (New York: Harper Perennial, 1996), p. 182.

AFFIRMATION OF FAITH

1. Nancy Gibbs and John F. Dickerson, "The Power and the Story," *Time* 154, no. 24 (December 13, 1999): 40.

2. Barbara Kingsolver, *Small Wonder* (New York: Perennial, 2002), p. xiii.

3. Ibid., p. 21.

4. *The Constitution of the Presbyterian Church (U.S.A.)* (Louisville: Office of the General Assembly, 1999), p. 268.

MIDDLE HYMN

1. Thank you to Jen Roberts for writing "You Can Sing" for this chapter.

2. Howard Rice and James C. Huffstutler, *Reformed Worship* (Louisville: Geneva, 2001), p. 206.

OFFERING

1. Michael L. Lindvall, *The Christian Life: A Geography of God* (Louisville: Geneva, 2001), p. 82.

2. Rainer Maria Rilke, *The Uncollected Poems of Rainer Maria Rilke*, translated by Edward Snow (New York: North Point, 1996), p. 127.

3. Erik H. Erikson, *Identity: Youth and Crisis* (New York: W. W. Norton, 1968), pp. 138–39.

PRAYERS OF THE PEOPLE

1. Jelaluddin Rumi, in *The Essential Rumi,* translated by Coleman Barks with John Moyne (New York: HarperCollins, 1995), p. 280.

2. *The Constitution of the Presbyterian Church (U.S.A.)* (Louisville: Office of the General Assembly, 1999), Directory for Worship, W-2.1002.

THE LORD'S PRAYER

1. Henri J. M. Nouwen, *Here and Now: Living in the Spirit* (New York: Crossroad, 1994), pp. 23–24.

SEALING

1. *The Constitution of the Presbyterian Church (U.S.A.)* (Louisville: Office of the General Assembly, 1999), Directory for Worship, W 1.3033 (2).

BAPTISM

1. Jelaluddin Rumi, in *The Essential Rumi*, translated by Coleman Barks with John Moyne (New York: HarperCollins, 1995), p. 172.

2. Rodger Nishioka, "Life in the Liquid Church: Ministry in a Consumer Culture," *Journal for Preachers* (Advent 2002): 31—36. Nishioka draws on the work of Pete Ward and Zygmunt Bauman.

3. Ibid, p. 31.

4. Tao Te Ching, translated by Stephen Mitchell (New York: Harper & Row, 1988), chapter 78.

5. Directory for Worship, W-2.3006.

6. See Matthew Fox, *Illuminations of Hildegard of Bingen* (Rochester, VT: Bear & Company, 2002), p. 43.

COMMUNION

1. Rainer Maria Rilke, *The Notebooks of Malte Laurids Brigge*, translated by Stephen Mitchell (New York: Vintage International, 1990), p. 20.

BEARING OUT

1. Seamus Heaney, *The Cure at Troy: A Version of Sophocles' 'Philoctetes'* (New York: Farrar, Straus and Giroux, 1961), pp. 77–78.

2. Ann Packer, *The Dive from Clausen's Pier* (New York: Knopf, 2002), p. 9.

3. Michael Lindvall, *The Christian Life: A Geography of God* (Louisville: Geneva, 2001), p. 59.

4. Used with permission from Eugenia Gamble.

CLOSING HYMN

1. Li-Young Lee, "You Must Sing," in *The City in Which I Love You* (Rochester, NY: BOA Editions, 1990), p. 69.

2. David R. Ray, *Wonderful Worship in Smaller Churches* (Cleveland: Pilgrim, 2000), p. 125.

BENEDICTION

1. Naomi Shihab Nye, "So Much Happiness," in *The Words Under the Words: Selected Poems* (Portland: Far Corner Books, 1995), p. 88. Used with permission of Naomi Shihab Nye.

AMEN

1. Tom Long, *Beyond the Worship Wars* (Bethesda: Alban Institute, 2001), p. 10.

2. Nigel Robb, *Let Everybody Say Amen* (St. Andrews, Scotland: St. Mary's College, 1994), p. 17.